DESTINY

DESTINY

A Generation Seeking God

Foreword by Dr. Rick E. Ferguson

Seth Jackson

VANTAGE PRESS
New York

Visit the author's website at www.godsdestiny.com

FIRST EDITION

Published by Vantage Press, Inc.
516 West 34th Street, New York, New York 10001

Manufactured in the United States of America
ISBN: 0-533-13769-1

Library of Congress Catalog Card No.: 01-130519

0 9 8 7 6 5 4 3 2 1

For mom and dad.
Thanks for standing by me, I love you.

Contents

Foreword

"Destiny"

Could this be the generation that finally finishes the job? Could this be the generation that completes the Great Commission, fulfills the prophetic plan and welcomes the return of King Jesus to planet earth? I think just maybe this is it . . . this is the generation that will finish the job.

Everywhere I look I am seeing an army of passionate God-chasers emerging from the current generation of students we often refer to as Gen-X. *Discover The Destiny* is a product of, and a ministry to this millennial generation. Seth Jackson is a part of the Gen-X culture. Seth Jackson is also a prophetic voice to the Gen-X culture. *Discover The Destiny* is a hard-hitting, no-retreat, take-no-prisoners, war-time manual designed to move an entire generation of serious, young disciples to the front lines of self-sacrifice, worship, and world-changing missions.

I believe this generation is ready to *discover the destiny*. God is moving thousands and thousands of young people into a lifestyle of spiritual adventure and reckless abandonment. These courageous young warriors are not looking to be entertained. They are absolutely appalled at anything plastic or staged. They could care less about well-polished religion. They are drawn magnetically to the authentic and the simple.

This generation of students is the most globally connected generation to ever live. They have a High-Tec chromosome no other generation has possessed. They have not been enslaved by the American dream. They are risk-takers, they are culturally savvy, they are entrepreneurial, they are hot, they are passionate, they are world-changers. They are truly ready to *discover the destiny*.

It is time we began to pour gas on the fire. This is a generation of people burning with a passion for genuine, unrestricted worship of the True and Living God. They are burning with a passion to follow Jesus to the ends of the world. They look at the 10-40 window and wonder why no one is jumping through this window. They are ignited by adventure and mission. This generation is burning with a hunger for biblical truth. Let's pour gas on the fire!!!

Discover The Destiny is gasoline to be poured on the fire. I pray that God will take what you are about to read and experience and use it to ignite a raging inferno of love for Him and irrevocable commitment to Him. If you are bored with mundane spiritual living . . . If you are ready jump with or without a parachute . . . If you feel it is time to move to the next level . . . If you are ready to go all the way with God . . . THEN . . . keep reading. It is time for you to *Discover The Destiny*.

—Dr. Rick E. Ferguson
Pastor, Riverside Baptist Church
Denver, Colorado

Acknowledgments

To my partners on the field of this ministry: Matt McGee and Brett Ferguson. I couldn't do this without you, and it's a pleasure sharing the journey with such great friends.

To the pastoral leadership that has guided us every step of the way: Mickey Ary, Menk Ferguson, Rick and Donna Shelton, Steve and Jacque DeShetler, Kurt Ervin, and Ed Callahan, thanks for the counsel and the encouragement.

To Wildwood Baptist Church, Russ Shinpoch, Wayne Collett, and Jeffrey Melvin: Thanks for believing, and putting feet to your faith by taking a chance and entrusting us with your teenagers' lives. Russ, especially to you, for reading a rough manuscript so many months ago, and saying it could become this book.

To my home church of First Baptist Church of Arnold, its pastor, Gerald Davidson, and all who have helped influence the pages of this book. A special note of thanks to the youth group of FBCA; it is your hearts that beat on the pages of this book . . . I love you guys.

To Jake Smith Jr., Chris Perstrope, Chris Lawrence, Josh Welker, and Steve Pullen . . . what can I say? Thanks for laughter and encouragement along the way.

To the Perstropes, one and all . . . where would I begin?

And finally, to Rick Ferguson. Your encouragement, your knowledge, and your heart have made this a reality. "Thank you" just doesn't seem to say enough. As Brett would say, "It's Worth It."

This book is dedicated to the memory of Lee Edward Perstrope.

Introduction

On April 20, 1999, I was spending the day preparing for an upcoming youth camp. I had just completed my tenure as an interim youth minister, and in just a few more weeks I would be returning to my "real" job. A tour would be starting soon with Barry Manilow (ask your mom, she will know who he is) and I was slated to design the staging and the lighting. After almost a year's hiatus, I was excited and looking forward to returning to the road. I had done my time with the youth ministry, but now it was time to get back to work . . . so I thought.

All afternoon I had heard bits of news about a suburban school in the Denver area that had experienced a school shooting. Though troubled by the news, I did the "Oh, my that's terrible" and moved on with my life. Little did I know how that day would forever change my view of this world.

When I finally reached a television set that evening I was shocked to see that the faces of the kids of Columbine were those of my kids. The same clothes, the same haircuts, the same tears. The school was like any of the three major schools in the area where I was living. The neighborhood was mine. Had God's divine plan for this life been different, it could have been Jefferson County, Missouri, instead of Jefferson County, Colorado.

As the days went on, I came to know people I had never met. Cassie Bernall, Rachel Scott, Corey DePooter, and a host of others became a part of my life. I sat numb in front of the television for days as the reality of what had happened began to sink in: God had allowed a line to be drawn in the sand. What would be our response? You see, the "why" and the "how" of Columbine is not the issue. Darrell Scott, whose daughter Rachel was killed at Columbine, told the Congress and the world the true reality of Columbine. I wonder how many of us were listening? "It was a spiritual event that should be forcing us to look at where the real blame lies!"

Columbine was not about the NRA. It was not about guns. It was not even about movies, television, or music. It was about a generation of young people who were headed down the road of believing they had no need of God. We have been so blessed in this country that we have forgotten what it means to need. We have grown up with cable television, computers, video games, and in our middle class world, we have had every need met. Our churches have become country clubs, and our youth groups have become activity planners. All of that changed on the 20th of April 1999. We saw the reality of life and death, not in a movie theater, but in a schoolyard, that looked like our own. We saw ourselves on the TV, not laughing and going about our daily lives, but covered with blood.

We live in an urgent time. As the government outlaws Jesus Christ in a methodical, step-by-step, manner, we have to go on the offensive. If we want to honor the memory of those precious lives lost at Columbine, then we had better start standing up for the Christ we claim to believe in. Nobody is going to hear our message if we keep it in the walls of our church. It is time we realize that the Jesus we serve today is not the sweet, mild, Jesus we read about in Matthew. Maybe we should be looking at the rest of the book. In Revelation, Jesus Christ is described as having "eyes of blazing fire," and a voice that was like "the sound of rushing waters." If we haven't figured it out, we ARE ashamed of the gospel. We hide in our church youth groups, scared to death of offending someone. We don't tell our friends at school about the One who has saved us and set us free. We have allowed the school to outlaw our Bible studies, stop our prayers, and beat us down until we are weak and useless. We gather around a flagpole for one morning every September and say we are "reaching" our schools . . . we should be ashamed. Keith Green said, "This generation of believers is responsible for this generation of souls" and that if the world is not being won, it's because "we're not doing it."

So many times in the wake of Columbine, people ask each other: "Would you have said 'yes,' if a gun were pointed at you?" How dare we even ask that question when we won't even tell our friends that Jesus loves them because we don't want to be laughed at! A girl who said "yes" in the face of a gun on April 20th was a girl who carried her faith boldly out in the open on April 19th. It is not the big, dramatic moments that make up your character, it is the everyday quiet opportunities to share Jesus that you let slip away that define who you are.

This book is a call to action. It is a book dedicated to the teenagers who have taught me so much in the last few years. It is the hope that this generation will be the one to say, "Enough is enough" and take a stand. If we don't heed the warning of Columbine; Springfield, Oregon; Heath High School, and countless others, what will it take to get our attention? When Christians stop being and preaching the truth, then the world is left to its own devices.

There is truth. There is right and wrong. There is a Savior. The hope of this book is that it will inspire you to pick up the torch that the people of Columbine have lighted. The fire has been started where their blood was shed. Will you let the flame go out, or will you spread the fire and start a revolution? Jesus doesn't have a lot of use for people who sit on the sidelines. In Revelation, he talks about the church of Laodicea. He tells them in chapter 3 that they are "neither hot nor cold" and therefore He is going to "spit them out of His mouth." Get in the game, or get off of the field. This book is designed to show you just how valuable a player you are.

DESTINY

Unique

As the end of my freshman year of high school approached, I began noticing signs up all over the school. The sign simply read, "PMA is coming." A crafty marketing approach, to be sure: nobody knew what it was, and everyone began making up all sorts of solutions to the mysterious acronym. As the weeks went on, it became known that the source of the mysterious message was the student council. Funny, I'm on student council, and I still don't know what this means!

After nearly a month, the mystery was revealed. The two student council sponsors had devised a program called, "Positive Mental Attitude"—duh, PMA. Once they got everyone talking about the plan, they decided to "let the cat out of the bag" and explain to us all just what this crazy thing was. They figured that all of the dances, spirit days, dress-up-like-whatever days, and pep rallies couldn't make any long-time difference in a teenager's life. Teaching teenagers that they were important, unique, and special could.

And teach it did. The program infused life back into the school. Discipline problems went down, grades improved, attendance at activities went through the roof, and everywhere you turned people were walking a little taller than they had before. The problem was that the energy couldn't be maintained. After a few months, the excitement of the program fell off, and things settled back to normal.

Why? How could something that was doing so much good for everyone just fade out? The reason is that for all of the right ideas contained in the program, they didn't give the students someone to believe IN. They told us we were special. They told us we were unique. They never told us "why." Without that vital ingredient, it is just hype. Hype fades away. God never does. Yes, you are unique. However, you cannot place those ideas into the context that you "evolved." You cannot place those ideas into the context that you were an "accident," or a "mistake." Only when you place the fact that you are special and unique BECAUSE you were created and finely crafted by a God who loves you, can you start to understand how truly special you are.

Inside each of us, God has planted the knowledge that we are unique and here on this earth for a higher purpose than just existing. Somewhere inside all of us, whether we believe in God or not, we have a sense that there is "something more." This is not just "human nature." This is caused by a deliberate act of God in His creation of you.

> He also has PLANTED ETERNITY IN MEN'S HEARTS AND MINDS (a divinely implanted sense of purpose working through the ages which nothing under the sun but God alone can satisfy) yet so that men cannot find out what God has done from the beginning to the end.
>
> —Ecclesiastes 3:11(Amplified)

You are unique, and you have a destiny because of what God has already deposited inside of you. Destiny is not about ambition, or gaining some great and lofty goal. You destiny is discovering the uniqueness of you, a treasure that has already been deposited inside of you since before you were born.

Psalm 139 says that God "knit us together in our mother's womb." He "created [our] inmost being." You were not the result of some collision of molecules. God cares for His creation, and He spends a great deal of thought and energy on everything he creates. You may have thought all of your life that you were just an "accident." Maybe you were the product of a rape, or a broken family. Perhaps you have been told that you were "worthless" or that you just don't matter. God is shouting out to you that you are not an accident. Man has accidents. God has creations. Even if you were the product of a rape, the rape didn't make you, God did. Psalm 139:14 says that we are "fearfully and wonderfully made." You are a prized creation to God. There is nothing about you that he didn't intend to be there.

This flies in the face of conventional wisdom. If the world can convince you that you are simply a mass of flesh and bone, without any character or soul, then Satan has opened the door to hundreds of falsehoods. If you are not a uniquely created being, then it is easy to believe that you need something more than what you are to be accepted. You need the right clothes, the right friends, or the right job to be worth anything. If you don't look like the people on TV, then you don't matter. Well, my God tells me in His word that I "was woven together in the depths of the earth," and that His eyes "saw my unformed body." All of us are unique, created, planned, and formed as individuals by a God who loves his creation.

Not only have the media, the government, and our society tried to destroy the reality of life, but they have destroyed thousands of lives as well. The lie of Planned Parenthood and the pro-abortion forces would tell us that a human life is only a fetus until it reaches a certain age. However, if you believe the word of God, you know without a doubt that God begins a life from the moment of conception, if not even before that. Psalm 130:15–16 says that "I was woven together in the depths of the earth, [God's] eyes saw my unformed body." Ephesians 1:4,5 says, "He chose us in Him before the foundation of the world, that we should be holy and blameless before Him. In love He predestined us to adoption as sons thorough Jesus Christ to Himself, according to the kind of intention of His will." When Jesus Christ was on the cross, He knew you. When God placed Adam in the garden of Eden, God already had plans for you. When God created the heavens and the earth, you were already in His plan. The Bible says, "He chose us from the foundation of the world." That is a long way from the first trimester.

Are you starting to see the picture? There are so many factors that have to combine to make you into a living, breathing person. It is not by accident, nor by chance. The sheer mathematics of it are astounding. Human life, all human life, is precious. You are a prized creation of God. Remember what David tells us in Psalms 139:

> O Lord, you have searched me and you know me. You know when I sit and when I rise; you perceive my thoughts from afar. You discern my going out, and my lying down, and you are familiar with all my ways. Before a word is on my tongue you know it completely.

God knows where you are, who you are, and where you are going. He has put you together with a specific role to play in His plan. Every thought, every action, every word uttered, is already known by God. The question is not "Why am I here?" The question is "What is your destiny for me?"

> . . . Declaring the end **and the result from the beginning,** and from ancient times the things that are not yet done, saying, My counsel shall stand, and I will do all My pleasure and purpose.
>
> —Isaiah 46:10

Here is how it comes together. God fulfilled his Plan for you from the beginning of your life. "For I know the plans I have for you" He tells us in His word. God is calling you out! God is saying to this generation "I have a plan for your life." If God has done all of this in your life, then it stands to reason that He has already equipped you with everything you need for the journey. If He knows where you are going, then He knows what you need in your bag to get there! Every talent, every ability, every physical characteristic, everything that is you, is there for a purpose along the journey!

Now the ball is in your court. When Jesus first came across the disciples they were living out their own lives. Jesus was walking beside the sea of Galilee, and He came across two brothers, Peter and Andrew. These two guys were fishermen. Since the beginning of the world, Jesus had known he would cross their path at this moment, and He knew what lay ahead for them. However, the choice had to be theirs. Jesus called to them, saying, "Come, follow me, and I will make you fishers of men." Notice what has happened here. God, the creator of these two men, didn't force them to go one way or another. They had a choice, and so do you. God has gifted us with a mind, and a will of our own. We don't have to entertain the plans of God. We can say "no," and go about our lives, ignoring God. Eventually, He will stop knocking at our heart's door, and give us over to a "depraved mind." But why on earth would you want to turn away from the road that you were created to follow? It is a waste of material to ignore the Master when He says "Come." We have the skills for the journey He calls us to. We have the personality for the people along the road whom He has planned for us to meet. If we ignore Him, if we turn away from the divine calling of Christ, then we have wasted all that we can be. Not only is God's grace so incredible that He would rescue a fallen race of people by sending His only Son to die on a cross as atonement for our sin. He also creates a wonderful, divine road through this life that will lead us, and, through our service, many others home to Him!

Learn the lesson of the apostles. When Jesus called them, the Bible says they "immediately" dropped their nets, left the boat, and followed after the King. They couldn't take their old life with them. This destiny required them to leave it all behind and start on a new path, the path that God had designed for them thousands of years before they were born. What nets are you still trying to hold onto? So often, we miss the incredible life that Steven Curtis Chapman so aptly phrased "the Great Adventure" by holding onto the nets when Jesus goes up the road. You can't hold onto the net, and you can't wait. Jesus won't stand still. The call of God keeps moving. You have this moment to rise up from the boat and go after God. Don't let the job, the boyfriend, or fear of embarrassment cause you to keep holding onto the net. You were created to be alive in this time, in the home where you are, in the school where you are. You were created to be the size you are, the color you are—the person you are. God has birthed a destiny inside of you. That destiny is waiting in a life given over to Him.

> . . . And who knows but that you have come to the kingdom for such a time as this.
>
> —Esther 4:14

Fulfilling the Destiny of You

Setting the spark . . . How many times have you found yourself thinking; "I can't do that"? The reasons are endless: I'm too young; I'm too old; I'm not smart enough; other people can do that, not me. The Bible says that God uses the "foolish things of the world to confuse the wise." What does that mean? It means that God created you the way you are, and He can use you, just as you are, to accomplish amazing things that will make the world wonder how it was done. The simple rule of life is lead, follow, or get out of the way. If you are ever caught saying "It can't be done," then you had better step out of the way for the person who is doing it. God is not impressed with our achievements. He is impressed with our faithfulness.

Read *1 Samuel 16: 1–13*

1. Samuel made several wrong choices for God's chosen one.

List the things that Samuel looked at as characteristics for leadership.

____

____

____

2. What did God say was the reason for choosing David?

____

____

Fanning the flame . . . When you are following the will of God, the world will try to tell you that you are lacking something. You don't have enough talent. You don't have enough money. We have never done it that way. If God has called you to something, and you know that you are seeking His heart and His will for your life, then faith is all that you need. When David went off to fight Goliath, he was stopped at every turn by a reason that he shouldn't stand up to Goliath, yet he knew God was with him, and because of his faith, he would succeed.

Read 1 Samuel 17:28–40.

List the arguments that each of the following made for David not to fight Goliath.

1. Eliab, David's oldest brother.

____

2. King Saul's first argument

____

3. King Saul's second argument

____

What was David's response to:

1. Eliab?
2. Saul in his first argument?
3. Saul in his second argument?

Igniting the passion . . . After diffusing everyone's doubts David then faced the taunts of Goliath. David's faith in the Lord held strong, even standing in front of the giant.

Read 1 Samuel 17:46–48.

After all of this, David didn't waste any time. The Bible says he ran to the fight with Goliath. God had promised, David believed, and he wasn't about to waste time on doubt. If the Lord says "go," then go. Don't hesitate, don't question, and don't give in to the doubts of others. The Lord has given you a purpose and a destiny. Go after it, believe in His power and not your own, and even the mountains can move.

Read Psalm 25, and make it your prayer as you go after the destiny God has given you.

Rescued

As a concert designer, I have had some pretty amazing experiences. I have traveled around the world and done nearly four hundred concerts in over 200 cities. I'm often asked what is it like to work with Don Henley, or Melissa Etheridge, and what my favorite city was. Usually, the conversation drifts into tales of being in Japan, or Europe, or Thailand. However, my most memorable city has nothing to do with a concert tour, but it holds my fondest memories of anywhere in the world: Bolivar, Missouri.

Where, you ask? Or perhaps more importantly, why? Bolivar is the location of Southwest Baptist University, and once a year, in early June, it becomes the location of a unique and very special camp called Super Summer. Super Summer is for Baptist teenagers from across the state that comes to spend a week in intense prayer, worship, and Bible study. Unlike other summer camps, there are no enticements like horseback riding, river raft trips, or water skiing. Super Summer is devoted to having a radical, life-changing encounter with Jesus Christ. Trying to explain this to someone can be difficult. If they ask you "what do you do there," the answer is "spend most of your day in classes or worship services." There are only a few hours of free time, and the rest of your day is devoted to worship and prayer. People usually look at you like you've lost your mind. "Teenagers go to camp . . . in the summer . . . to attend classes and pray?" The thing that can't be described is being in the presence of God. It is something that those who have experienced it easily understand, and those who haven't struggle to make sense of the passion that it stirs in you.

The camp is broken down into age groups. You spend the day in your "school," and within that age group you have a "family" group with a "mom and a pop". The moms and pops are usually college or graduate students who serve as adult leaders during the week. Each family group has between twelve and fifteen teenagers in it, and each school has a worship leader and two "deans." This particular year, one of the family groups contained a sixteen-year-old named Eric. Eric was quiet, and it was painfully obvious that he had been forced to come to camp. Eric always sat in the back, and was basically silent for most of the week. The people in his group said he came from a rough home. Though he wouldn't share any of his life with those of us at the camp, you could see a life of pain written in his face.

The final night of camp, I was delivering a message that has become the basis for this book. God finally broke through to Eric. As the service was finishing, Eric was sobbing uncontrollably. His family group had gathered around him, and they were praying and talking with him. I sat back and watched the miracle of all miracles occur right before my eyes. Eric had finally realized how important he was to God. That Jesus loved him. That despite the life that he had been placed in, God had so much more for him. That night, his friends led him into a personal relationship with Jesus Christ. The baggage of sixteen years was released, and Eric began his life over again. Nothing in the world can replace the look in the face of someone who has just met Christ. I sat there, wanting to hold onto this moment forever. The joy in Eric's face, the amazement and euphoria of the friends who led him to the Lord, it was unforgettable.

Jesus knew this. His last instructions to His church before he left were to reach out into the world and lead others to the same life that had been offered to them. Tell people about how Jesus came into this world to rescue what would be unreachable without the sacrifice Jesus made for us. In a recent survey, however, we find that most of us are not following the last instructions given to us. In fact, only ten percent of the people in this nation who claim to be Christians actually have led someone to a personal relationship with Christ! What are the other ninety percent doing? We are doing exactly what God told us not to. In Matthew 5:15, 16, Jesus tells us that we shouldn't "light a lamp and put it under a bowl. Instead they put it on its stand, and it gives light to everyone in the house. In the same way, let your light shine before men, that they may see your good deeds and praise your Father in heaven." Jesus loves us. He reached across eternity to save us from our own sin and failures. What do we do with what He has done for us? We hide.

Embracing your destiny, however, calls you to a different place. Your destiny lies in following Jesus Christ, wherever he may lead. That carries with it a cost. He says in His word that we have to DAILY "take up OUR cross and follow Him. . . ." He didn't say go to one camp. He didn't say just go to church on Sunday and everything will be fine. He said daily . . . every day. We have to live out what we claim has changed every part of our lives. Remember that God has given us a destiny and a purpose, but He also has given us a mind and a will of our own. God won't force you to do anything. He didn't make a race of robots. He made a wonderful creation that sin has tarnished. His only Son came into this world, a perfect, sinless sacrifice for us. With the price of Jesus dying on the cross, our debt was erased. With His resurrection from the grave, we have a living, powerful king who waits to support us, rescue us, and love us. The choice to receive or reject this gift is ours. Once we have accepted Jesus, He asks something of us. You can't earn His love. You can't pay for your salvation. You can, however, share the joy of it with others.

"Witnessing" as the church code word calls it, is one of the simplest, yet most frightening, experiences of the Christian life. Satan knows that a Christian with a powerful witness and desire to see their friends and family to be set free can do tremendous damage to his kingdom. That is why he spends so much of his energy to stop us from sharing Jesus with the rest of the world. On the grand scale, governments all over the world block missionaries from coming into the lands. People go to some of the most remote parts of the world, simply because Jesus said "follow me." Often they are killed, or tortured. Many have simply vanished. In our world, we are held hostage by a fear that people will think we are freaks. One of the greatest human fears is to not be accepted. We have to feel like we belong somewhere, and the fear that people will reject us or make fun of us can freeze us in our tracks.

But you do belong! If you are a Christian you belong to the greatest family the world has ever known. God knew how scary this world could be. Jesus walked through it just like we are. That is why God gives us His Holy Spirit as a constant companion. From the moment you accept Jesus Christ into your life, God takes up residence in you. He becomes a part of your heart, your mind, and your life.

God then begins working out opportunities for you to share what He has done in you with others. For those ninety percent who never witness, it is not that they haven't had the chance, they have just chosen to ignore the opportunity. God places people and opportunities in our lives every day. Our main destiny as Christians is not to be rich, or achieve some mighty goal, it is to lead others, a person at a time, home to Jesus. You cannot grow in your relationship with Christ without witnessing. You cannot achieve and discover your destiny without witnessing. It is critical to the Christian life. To sin by silence, is still a sin. How many times have we felt that pulling in our hearts and backed down? Is it easy? No. Is it critical? Yes.

We have to open up our eyes and start seeing this world as Jesus saw it. If we can get a God's-eye view of the people around us then can become like the prophet Jeremiah. This guy risked his life every time he opened his mouth. He knew that the message of God was black and white. He knew that God's word didn't give a place for gray. It was either God's way, or it was sin. He never pulled a punch, either. Just to give you an idea of his intensity, take a look at Jeremiah 6. Jeremiah tells the people that they "have no shame at all," that they "don't even know how to blush," that they will "fall among the fallen," that they are "greedy" and that the word of the Lord is "offensive" to them. Was he scared? Probably. Did he back down? Not at all. In chapter 20 he says "his word is in my heart like a fire, a fire shut up in my bones. I am weary of holding it in; indeed, I cannot."

God gives us a fire that we cannot hold in! Has Jesus done anything for you? Has he set you free? Has he restored something that was broken? Has he set you free? Has he given you a destiny? Has he given you life? If Jesus has done anything in your life, then you have a message that a lost and dying world is desperate to hear! In case you haven't noticed your generation is fed up with professional religion. They are fed up with families that fall apart. They are fed up with friends who let them down. They are fed up with leaders who lie and cheat. They are fed up with a world that tells them the road to happiness is looking a certain way, or wearing a certain label. They are fed up with a school society that locks them into a group and labels them jock, or Goth, or burnout. You hold in your heart the message that tells them they are unique, special, and covered in a life that sin that can be wiped away in an instant by a God that has known them since before they were born! Let it be a fire in your bones that you cannot hold in!

We have to see our world as Jesus saw it. In Matthew 9:35, it says that Jesus,

> Went through all of the towns and villages, teaching in their synagogues, preaching the good news of the kingdom and healing every disease and sickness. When he saw the crowds, he had compassion on them, because they were harassed and helpless, like sheep without a shepherd.

Love always motivated the actions of Jesus. He didn't look

into a crowd of people and see drunks, or prostitutes, or liars, or cheats. He saw sheep without a shepherd. He saw people that were covered in sin, and lost. A people that had no idea how amazing they really were, and how they had a unique place in God's kingdom if only they would find Him. Jesus never saw people in terms of labels, prestige, or power. It says He was "moved with compassion." Why? Because he saw them as harassed. The original translation uses a word that means they were tired, frustrated, bored, empty and lifeless. They had looked for happiness in every way, and all of it had left them empty and lonely. It also says they were "helpless." They were wandering through life without any purpose. They had spent their whole lives trying to find that "groove" or track that would fit and allow everything to make sense. They had tried different types of relationships, different types of sins, anything to fill that sense of eternity that is inside all of us.

Now, I don't know about you, but that describes most people I meet every day. Yet there we sit, each and every day with the answer, and we keep it to ourselves because we are scared of what might happen to our precious reputations.

When I was a senior in high school, I took an art class. I thought it would be a good way to fill a credit without having to put up much effort, and most of the people in the room were there for the same reason. We spent most of the class talking about where we were going to college, who we were dating, and what was happening after homecoming. The teacher, Mrs. Johnson, was a great lady who really loved her teenagers, and we all had a great time together. That one particular Friday in October started out like any other. We all arrived for class, excited about the upcoming weekend, starting our usual discussions about who was going with whom, and where everyone would be this weekend. About ten minutes into the class, the principal came by and pulled Mrs. Johnson out into the hall. A moment later, they both came back into the room, both crying. The principal, Mr. Hall, was visibly shaken, and found it difficult to speak. Quietly, he said that Mike, a boy in this very class, was dead. It seems that this sophomore came home, went into the garage, started the car, and sat down to await his death. Everyone was shocked. For the entire hour, very little was said, and everyone just sat and stared at the empty desk that, only yesterday, had been filled by a quiet little kid who would never come to class again.

I wish I could say that I knew Mike. I wish I could say that I had seen this hurting kid, and as a senior, chose to reach out and encourage him. I wish I could, but I can't. What I can say, is that I spent that hour not grieving for Mike, but trying desperately to even recall what he looked like. The truth is, I didn't ever speak to him. I didn't ever smile at him. I didn't even look at him long enough to know his face, and he sat right next to me. In fact, as the weeks went by, I learned that he lived two streets away from me and even rode the same bus I was on. Yet it took until the yearbook came out that spring before I ever saw his face. Even then, I still didn't remember him.

I think of Mike often. I held the answer to his questions. I had the key to healing his hurts. I had everything that makes life worth living, and not once did I bother to stop and look around. I wasted two months of divine opportunities sitting in a class trying to impress football players and cheerleaders while a quiet, hurting life slipped away. His life was entrusted to my care, and I didn't even bother to notice he was even alive. I pray that someday in heaven, I will see Mike . . . but I doubt that I will. Mike was a soul I was responsible for, and now he is gone. What would five minutes out of my life to reach out to a hurting heart done for his eternity? I wonder.

Every day there are kids like Mike who decide that life just isn't worth living, and step out of this world. Somewhere in the United States, students are planning on killing other students in their school. We live in a world where life and death have become a reality to teenagers. How can we keep silent? How can we hold in the fire that is burning in our bones? It doesn't take a great preacher to win the lost. It doesn't take a big church, or big events. Our church Wednesday night services and our pizza parties are never going to reach out to a hurting world. It takes you. It takes a willing heart. We have to start seeing this world as our Lord sees it. We have to have a passion for the lost. We have to stop kidding ourselves into believing that there is always going to be another day, and that maybe hell isn't real. We aren't guaranteed one more breath on this earth. The Bible tells us that life is "but a vapor" and that hell is very real. Jesus said, "I am the way, the truth, and the life," and no one comes to know God or have the security of knowing they are going to heaven apart from Jesus Christ. The Holy Spirit, living inside of you, is hard at work providing opportunities for you. What will you do with the life God has given you?

> I am obligated both to Greeks and non-Greeks, both to the wise and the foolish. That is why I am so eager to preach the gospel also to you who are at Rome. I am not ashamed of the gospel, because it is the power of God for the salvation of everyone who believes. . . .
>
> —Romans 1:14–16 (NIV)

Fulfilling the Destiny of Evangelism

Setting the spark . . . We are all called to be witnesses of what Jesus has done in our lives. Just as someone introduced you to Jesus: a parent, a friend, a brother or sister, we are to share the hope that we have found. Jesus gave us this as a command, so there is no need to pray about whether or not God has called you to witness. You are called. Sadly, only a handful of the people in this nation who call themselves a Christian, have ever witnessed. Why? Because the devil knows what kind of damage a person can do to his control if they start leading people to Jesus. We are scared of wit-

nessing. We are fearful of what the world will think or say about us. As a result, we simply do nothing.
Read Matthew 28: 16–20.

1. What has God called us to be?

   ____

2. What is God's promise to us as His witnesses?

   ____

Fanning the flame . . . Remember when you first became a Christian? You had an unquenchable fire. You couldn't wait to tell everyone you knew what had happened in your life. Where has that fire gone? If we are going to find our destiny, then we have to have the passionate, infectious love of God that spills into every area of our life. Witnessing is not some procedure. It is who you are. You are a witness. You either reflect the love of Christ, or you reflect the world.

Read Hebrews 10:32–39.

1. What is it that we have thrown away?

   ____

2. Why is it we were willing to be persecuted? What knowledge did we possess?

   ____

3. Why should we not be those who shrink back?

   ____

List three instances where you felt ashamed and hid from an opportunity to be a witness.

1. ____
2. ____
3. ____

Igniting the passion . . . The Bible says that the early church turned the world "upside down" (Acts 17:6). Their message, preached by a small group of people, was shouted to such volume, that the whole world was affected by it. Wearing a T-shirt or having a bumper sticker with a fish on it is not an effective witness. The point of being a witness is being able to bring people into a relationship with Jesus. It is critical, it is essential, and God commands us to do it. We cannot be ashamed of Christ. If we are, then we don't really believe that He has the power the Bible says. If we can't believe that, then we have to wonder if we are even saved. Every day, opportunities to witness pass by me. Often, I am reminded of them in my quiet times with God. Be focused, be bold, and always be ready to tell someone the most incredible hope they can ever know.

Read Romans 1:16.

Memorize this verse, then make it your prayer to God. Pray that you would never forget that the message of Jesus carries the power to change someone's life. No book, video, song, or person can do that. Only Jesus Christ can save.

Holy

In my early teens, I used to live for that special week known as "youth camp." Every year, my church would take about seventy teens, from seventh grade to twelfth grade off to the Ozark Mountains to a place called Windermere. Every year the plan was the same. My friends and I would begin the planning about a month out, for all of our camp activities. Now, I'm talking about swimming, diving, and basketball. I'm talking about the covert, after-hours activities that made camp "the" place to be. We would pack up our camping gear, camouflage, flashlights, and head out with all of our secret plans. I don't remember us doing anything but eluding the night security patrols, but it was the thrill of the chase that drove us on. The other activity that everyone knew would happen, but didn't really require any planning, was the "Thursday night rededication." Every year it was the same. You would spend every night sneaking around the woods, every day skipping the morning bible classes, and every afternoon playing around in the lake. Then in the evening, you would dive into the ten tons of luggage that you brought for five days, pull out your best "pimp-daddy" look, and head off to the evening service. The evening service was about being seen, and you had to look your best if you were going to impress the girls. Did I forget to mention God in all of this? That is because we forgot to pay attention to Him. That is, until Thursday night.

Thursday night was always the night geared to the emotional response. The pastor hit it home, the music was aimed to create the most emotional state they could stir up, and it was usually the night they would show the hard-hitting video about suicide or drunk driving. By the end of the evening, everyone in the room was in tears, flying down to the altar, and committing their lives to follow God, surrender to the ministry, and win their school to Christ that fall. It was always one of those defining moments. You know the times when you let your friends see you cry, and hug everyone who will come within ten feet of you. You head out of the service into some small group and stare up at the night sky, talking about how amazing God is, and how great the week has been, and how special being with Christian friends is. The next day, you go home ready to storm the gates of hell.

There is only one problem. After about a week, the "only Christian music" oath you made starts to fade away with the release of every new hit song. After about two weeks, the "I'm going to read my Bible every day" oath has faded to about once every three days. Little by little, the old life returns and before school starts, it was like we had never been to camp at all.

Why? How is it that a commitment that you are so focused on can't be kept after only a few weeks? The answer is simple to hear, but difficult to accept: you don't really want to change.

> You yourselves are God's temple and that God's Spirit lives in you . . . If anyone destroys God's temple, God will destroy him; for God's temple is sacred, and you are that temple.
>
> —Corinthians 3:16–17

Throughout the Bible, God always focused on the condition of His temple. When the Israelites were wandering around the desert, no matter what, whenever they set up camp, they made sure the tent that was the temple was assembled. God's presence dwelt inside that temple. That is why the Ark of the Covenant was so important to them. It was the representation of God's power to the Israelites. Today, we don't need a temple or an ark. After Jesus was raised from the dead, He gave us the Holy Spirit to be His presence on the earth. That Holy Spirit lives inside of every one who has accepted Jesus Christ as their savior. When Jesus died on the cross and rose from the dead, he completed everything we need. In 2 Corinthians 1:19–20, Paul tells us that Christ became the "yes" and the "amen" to all of our needs. The word "yes" is pretty self-explanatory, and "amen" means "in strong agreement with." God promised salvation to his people and Jesus came and said, "I am the salvation." God promised to meet all of our needs and Jesus came and said, "I am the vine, you are the branches, and he that abides in me bears much fruit." He is our sufficiency, our completion, and our total need. When we are saved, we receive everything God has to offer! The Holy Spirit takes up residence in us, and we become the very temples of God, because God is now dwelling inside of us.

As a result, God is very particular about how is temple is treated. The Bible says that God cannot be present where there is sin. If your life is full of garbage, then your temple has no room for God to do his work. God's temple is serious business. As a result, the contents of your heart are of serious business to God. In Matthew 21: 12–16 we see a picture of the intensity that God views His temple. Jesus enters the temple, and is outraged at everything that is going on in the temple. People are selling goods and services, and the church has become big business. Jesus, however, had seen enough. "He overturned the tables of the moneychangers, and the benches of those selling doves. 'It is written,' he said to them, 'My house will be called a house of prayer, but you are making it a den of robbers.' "

Now don't miss the importance of this picture. None of these people were doing anything really "wrong." The moneychangers were there because the temple in those days used its own form of money. As a result, these guys were doing a service by exchanging Roman currency for the temple currency. Also, people in the temple needed to make sacrifices as atonement for sin. So, there were traders there in the courts that would sell people doves for the sacrifices. They weren't doing anything wrong, they were providing a service, right? God says "no." His temple is dedicated to prayer and worship. If we start clogging up the entrance to the temple with all of the junk the world has to offer, no matter how useful, we stop the temple from being the temple, and God may have to overturn a few things.

What is in your temple? How many things have you placed at the temple gates that distract you from your true purpose? In our culture today, activity has reached new levels. We have sports practice, dances, recitals, church activities, homework, school activities, jobs, dates, and once in awhile, we even see our family. Where is God in all of this? Our lives only have so much room. If we put God at the bottom of the list we won't get to Him. You cannot make room for God. You have to give Him the priority. "Seek FIRST the kingdom of God and His righteousness, and all of these things will be added to you." Give God your first effort, and everything else will fall into place. Have your quiet time first thing in the morning, because if you wait till after Letterman, your brain is so fried, you don't know who you are praying to. Make church a priority. Don't let a job or some sport stop you from spending time worshiping Him. Don't waste hour after hour watching TV or playing Sega, then wonder why you can't stay close to God.

The Bible says, "where your heart is, there your treasure will be." Where is your treasure? The best judge of your relationship with Jesus is where you invest your time and your money. Your brain is the most amazing computer ever created. Yet it only is as good as what is put into it. We need to be very aware of what we allow into our minds. The time we spend in front of the TV, listening to the wrong kinds of music, or surfing through the wrong types of websites, is wasted. Those hours are gone, and we will never get them back. Slowly and methodically, you are allowing your temple to become a den of robbers. Eventually, God will have had enough and He will take action to clean his temple.

How does God want us to live? He gives us some powerful guidelines in the third chapter of Colossians. Verse 2 says that we must "set our minds on Christ." This doesn't just mean a one-time choice. This is not a decision that can be made at camp, and then you are done. The amplified bible puts it this way: "set your minds, and keep them set, on what is above (the higher things), and not what is on the earth." This is the answer to the most-asked questions in youth ministry: "Should I see that movie?" "Should I listen to this band?" "Is that really bad?" We must continue to set our minds on Christ. If you are going to fulfill your destiny in Christ, then you have no room for the things of this world. You must continue to "keep your mind set" on the things of God. So, is that movie bad? I don't know. Does it pull your mind from the direction Jesus wants you to go? It is a hard-line approach to life. Sadly, with only 10 percent of the church even bothering to share their faith, it is up to you to stand in the gap. That takes courage, commitment, and a constant commitment to keep your temple a house of prayer.

Second, we must set our hearts on Christ:

> If then you have been raised with Christ (to a NEW LIFE, sharing His resurrection from the dead) aim at and seek the rich, eternal treasures that are above, where Christ is, seated at the right hand of God.
>
> —Colossians 3:1 (Amplified)

Jesus has given us a new life. He has made us a part of Him. If the Holy Spirit is dwelling in our hearts, then we need to make sure our hearts are focused on this NEW LIFE that comes from Jesus! That means our friendships, our job, how we dress, the places we go ALL must reflect that new life that is in Christ. You can't be a witness to a room full of drunks. "But I'm not drinking, so I can go to those parties and be a witness." Uhhhh, no. The Bible says that we have been resurrected from that life. If you are alive, then you have no business hanging around with a bunch of corpses. The Holy Spirit is dwelling in you! Why would you drag Him back into the pits?

We must put to death anything associated with your earthly nature.

> So kill, (deaden, deprive of power) the evil desire lurking in your members (those animal impulses and all that is earthly in you that is employed to sin): sexual **vice, impurity, sensual appetites, unholy desires, and all greed and covetousness for that is idolatry (the deifying of self and other created things instead of God).**
>
> —Colossians 3:5

Fulfilling the Destiny of Holiness

Setting the spark. . . .

Read 1 Corinthians 3:16–17

1. We are God's ______________________.
2. God's ______________________ lives in you.
3. God's temple is ______________________.

How many times have you gone to a great service, or come to a camp or retreat, and got all fired up to live for God? How many days or weeks did it take till you fell right back into your old habits? Maybe we should ask ourselves what we have in OUR temple! The Holy Spirit of God is not going to hang out where sin abounds!

Read Matthew 21:12–16.

Jesus is coming into your temple this week. What will he find? Will He find a clean, orderly temple that is seeking after Him? Or will he find a place that has been filled up with the world's trash, and there is no room to get anything done for God?

In the Old Testament, people used to have to build a place for the Spirit of God. That was what the Ark of the Covenant was all about. The presence of God was carried around by the Israelites. After Jesus was taken up into heaven, he left his people the Holy Spirit to live and dwell inside of each everyone that accepts Him as savior. That being the case, WE become the temples of God! As a result, God expects us take care of His temple!

Fanning the flame. . . .

We need to live lives that reflect that Spirit of God inside of us. "God is Holy, therefore, we must be Holy." He wants the old stuff out, and His new stuff in!

Read Colossians 3.

This is a powerful chapter. This is your guide to living. There are three main things we have to do in order to keep our temple in order.

1. *We must* set our minds on Christ. *Verse 2 in the Amplified Bible says that we should* set our minds AND KEEP THEM SET on what is above (the higher things), not on the things that are on the earth.

What are some things on the earth that I need to quit thinking about?

1. ______________________________
2. ______________________________
3. ______________________________

What are some of the "higher things" that I should be focused on?

1. ______________________________
2. ______________________________
3. ______________________________

2. *We must set our* hearts on Christ. *Again, the Amplified Bible says in vs.* 1 If then you have been raised with Christ (to a NEW LIFE, sharing His resurrection from the dead) aim at and seek the rich, eternal treasures that are above, where Christ is, seated at the right hand of God. *Jesus has given us a new life. He has made us a part of Him. If the Holy Spirit is dwelling in our hearts, then we need to make sure our hearts are focused on this NEW LIFE that comes from Jesus!*

3. *We must put to death anything associated with your earthly nature. Vs. 5 in the Amplified Bible puts it in pretty direct terms:*

So kill, (deaden, deprive of power) the evil desire lurking in your members (those animal impulses and all that is earthly in you that is employed to sin): sexual **vice, impurity, sensual appetites, unholy desires, and all greed and covetousness for that is idolatry (the deifying of self and other created things instead of God.)**

What does that entire mean? It means that we need to get rid of those things that take the place of God as the controlling factor of our lives. When we let those things get control of us we make ourselves, or something else in this world our god. Basically, we let the salesmen into the temple. Do that, and Jesus is going to clean it up . . . the HARD WAY!

What are some things in my temple that need to be swept out?

1. ______________________________
2. ______________________________
3. ______________________________

(Use the extra note pages at the end of the book if you need more room!)

Ignite your destiny. . . .

So you've got yourself all cleaned up, right? Well, what have you put in its place? If you don't fill up your life with God, you are going to fall right back into the same place where you were!

Read Matthew 12:43–45.

Prayerful

Ever since I can remember, prayer has been a part of my life. We pray before meals, we pray in church, we pray before the football game. It wasn't until a few years ago, however, that I understood prayer. I was helping to lead a camp with my good friend, Kurt, a youth pastor working in a small town in southern Missouri. I hadn't really spent much time with Kurt since we were kids, and my impression of him was still based in that frame of mind. I, however, was in for a surprise. I was assigned to work under Kurt for the week. Admittedly, I was more excited about catching up with an old friend than catching the fire of God. The first night was pretty basic. We got acquainted with everyone, got to know the students, played a couple of games, and sent everyone on their way. Kurt, as I saw it, was still Kurt.

The next night, however, things began to look different to me. Kurt was delivering a message on holiness, and God's presence was thick in the room. It was almost a visible cloud. God was working and moving in the hearts of these students as Kurt preached, as a man possessed of God. As he reached the invitation, the room was in tears. All over the room, students were broken, sobbing, coming face to face with God. I sat stunned. I had never witnessed anything like this. One by one, students came up and confessed sins that I couldn't believe they would utter in public. One young man slowly made his way up to the microphone. He told an unbelievable tale of drug addiction, theft, and alcohol abuse. He said that God was setting him free, and that he wanted to know Jesus. I felt the hair standing up on the back of my neck, as right in front of me, I watched this genuine, broken teenager ask Jesus into his life. I was so excited; I couldn't believe the miracles that were happening all around me. Then, suddenly I was terrified. Kurt had just called my name. Why? I walked to the front, sheepishly, wondering what on earth I was about to do. I wasn't used to this! Though exciting, this was not my nice, dignified church service. This was real confession, real tears, real repentance, and a very real Holy Spirit doing an amazing work in the room. He told me he wanted me to pray with him over this young man who had just been saved and needed deliverance from drug and alcohol abuse. What? I kept thinking, "wait here, while I go find you someone spiritual; I can't do this."

But Kurt knew there was more being developed than this man's life. God was about do a work in mine as well. We began to pray, or I should say Kurt began to pray. I stood dumbfounded. Then I realized what was happening. My hand was on this teen's shoulder and I began to feel him shudder. He was crying uncontrollably as the prayers continued. Little by little, God was ripping away layers of pain and hurt from this guy's life. Suddenly, I felt energized. Specific areas of sin came to mind, and I began calling them out one by one. Praying with as much energy as I could muster, I felt an intensity and burden for this young man like I had never known. I cried, I begged, I prayed with a passion I cannot describe, and when it was over, an hour had gone by.

That night, I realized that there was a big difference between "Now I lay me down to sleep," and "God, break me." "Lord, bless this food" doesn't cut it against "Lord, use me for your will." Since that night, I have learned that prayer, real prayer, is never just a phrase or list of wants. Prayer is always powerful, always life changing, always deep and always focused or isn't prayer at all.

The problem is, in a country where we have every blessing we could imagine, we don't know what it is to need. Even at America's worst, we still have no comprehension of the kind of poverty and pain that many people in the world go through. As a result, we are spoiled in our prayer life. We find ourselves having too many blessings and too little appreciation. As Christians, we are in no danger of being killed for our beliefs. So often, if our beliefs are even challenged we simply back down, and hide out. Powerful prayer, sadly, is a distant memory to most of our churches.

We tend to think of prayer as a way to get what we want, to show off our spirituality, or to simply make ourselves feel better about our pathetic attempts at being the church Christ has called us to. We have forgotten that prayer is our greatest weapon, our very link to God, and God's precious gift to allow us communication with Him. If this generation is going to fulfill its destiny for Christ then we have to start believing that prayer is powerful, effective and critical. It is not something we do out of tradition or habit, it is the very key to our survival. Jesus tells us in Mark 11:22,

> Have faith in God. I tell you the truth, if anyone says to this mountain, "Go, throw yourself into the sea," and does not doubt in his heart but believes that what he says will happen, it will be done for him. Therefore I tell you, whatever you ask for in prayer, believe that you have received it, and it will be yours. And when you stand praying, if you hold anything against anyone, forgive him, so that your Father in heaven may forgive you your sins.

The early church had a belief and a faith that reacted like this. In Acts 12: 5–7, Peter was in prison. Was he calling Johnnie Cochran? No, the Bible says "so Peter was kept in prison, BUT the church was earnestly praying to God for him." Peter is in prison. Does that matter? No. Why? "Peter was in prison, BUT the church was earnestly praying for him." There was no doubt in the word of God. There was no "I hope he gets out, maybe we should pray." The church was earnestly praying and God was listening. That night the angels had a prison break. Peter was busted out of the jail and out of the city that night by an angel, and the guards were so stunned they thought they were hallucinating. The important thing is that the prayer the Bible speaks of here is not the kind of prayers we see in our churches today. These people were focused, committed, and faithful. They believed God, and they weren't moving until he showed Himself. In verse 12, Peter returns home. The Bible says it is the NEXT morning and that there were "many people [who] had gathered and were praying." They didn't just pray for ten minutes and quit. They understood that prayer is real, prayer is powerful, and that their God is Almighty, Prince of Peace, and Lord of Lords! They didn't hesitate. They didn't doubt. They hit their knees, and they stayed there. Peter was arrested during the Passover week. It was King Herod's intention to put him on trial after the holiday was over. Peter's jailbreak happened on the night before his trial. So it is safe to assume that these people didn't just pray for a couple of hours. We are talking DAYS, here. Imagine, days of prayer. How often do we fall asleep ten minutes into our quiet time, and then wonder why God never seems to be an active part of our lives?

"But I prayed really hard, and God didn't do it. My life is still in shambles." God never promises us everything we want. He tells us in James 4:3 that our motives have to be right. That, coincidentally, comes from prayer. When we spend our time in prayer, we develop a close relationship with God. When we have God's heart as our motive, our prayers reflect His will. Look at the life of David. David was the only person God said was a "man after God's own heart." David wrote most of the Psalms and was in a constant state of communication with God. He was a king, a hero, and wealthy. But everything was not perfect in David's world. He committed murder and adultery, his own son tried to kill him, and he eventually lost his kingdom. Through it all though, he was holding on tight to his relationship with God. Read the words of his Psalms and you get a sense of the openness and honesty that true prayer can be, even in the hardest of times. In Psalm 31: 9 he says, "Be merciful to me, O Lord, for I am in distress; my eyes grow weak with sorrow, my soul and my body with grief. My life is consumed with anguish and my years by groaning." David was alone, hurting and defeated. He talks of a "physical affliction." Did he give up or get mad at God? Did he stop praying and having a quiet time, saying that "I gave God a chance but nothing happened"? No. In the very same chapter he declares long, loud, and strong: "Praise be to the Lord, for he showed his wonderful love to me.... Love the Lord, all his saints! The Lord preserves the faithful ... be strong and take hope in the Lord!"

Prayer is the fuel that drives us onward, keeps us going, and picks us up when the world falls down around us. "But you don't understand what I've been through!" It doesn't matter what you have been through; a powerful, active prayer life will take you through it all. The old hymn says it best: "Everything to God in prayer!" The problem is that, so often, we let laziness, sin, and our own pride destroy our prayer life. Isaiah 59 puts the whole issue into perspective.

> Surely the arm of the Lord is not too short to save, nor his ear too dull to hear. But your iniquities have separated you from your God; your sins have hidden his face from you, so that he will not hear. For your hands are stained with blood, your fingers with guilt. Your lips have spoken lies, and your tongue mutters wicked things.

When our hearts aren't focused on seeking and knowing God, our prayer life is motivated in the wrong direction, if it occurs at all, and our prayers become silent and ineffective.

Israel had this problem over and over again in the Bible. They had seen God do amazing miracles for them. They had been witnesses to the most magical stories of the Bible. Unfortunately, they had many times where they ignored God and allowed themselves to start thinking they could get the job done on their own. They would make excuses for their sin, and they would do all of the actions necessary to make themselves they were spiritual. They would even have these public displays of prayer, making outlandish requests of God. Sounds like most churches in America today. We are no different, and our prayer lives are equally as ineffective. We go to church week after week, put in our time, and leave no different than when we arrived. We can be so spiritual on Sunday nights, but come Monday morning, we leave behind all evidence of Christ in our lives. We are ashamed of God and his Son, and yet we have the nerve to shout out and worship Him on a Sunday morning. I'm not sure God is listening. In Amos he tells the people to take "away the noise of your songs." "I cannot stand your assemblies. . . . I will not listen to the music of your harps." We have become the church and the generation that God speaks of in Revelation as the church that He will "vomit out of his mouth," because they were neither hot nor cold. A church, a youth group, a person has become so disgusting to God that he would vomit when we become a group of people whose worship and prayer lives are a sham. God asks the question, "These men have set up idols in their hearts, and put wicked stumbling blocks before their faces. Should I inquire of them at all?" Author J. B. Phillips wrote that

> We cannot help feeling disturbed as well as moved, for this surely is the church as it was meant to be. It is vigorous, flexible, for these are the days before it ever became fat and short of breath through prosperity. These men did not make "acts of faith," they simply believed. They did not "say a prayer," they really prayed. If these men were naïve by modern standards, we have to admit that they were open to the God side of things in a way almost unknown today.

Prayer is communication with God. It is listening as well as speaking. An active prayer life comes from the desire to know your God. When we call on Him with a pure and seeking heart, when we really want to find Him, he promises to be there:

> . . . This is the confidence we have in approaching God! If we ask anything according to his will, he hears us. And if we know that he hears us—whatever we ask—we know that we have what we asked of him.
>
> —1 John 5:14

James says, "We do not have, because we do not ask." That word, "ask," in the Greek, translates, "to crave." You don't have, because you don't crave! In Exodus, Moses had been in the desert for three days without any water. Now, the human body can't make it much longer than that without water, so things were pretty desperate. They finally reached a town, but their water was bitter and it couldn't be used. So, true to form, the Israelites panic. They cry out at Moses to fix the problem. Moses turns to prayer. The Bible says that he "cried out" to God. In the Greek translation, it is the same word used to describe what the Israelites felt when they saw the entire Egyptian army coming at them. That is desperate. We are talking a life-and-death fear. I imagine this was no "O Lord, thou art so wonderfulleth" type of prayer. It was probably sweet, simple, and to the point: "GOD! WE NEED YOU!" God delivered. He told Moses to throw a piece of wood into the water, and the water became purified enough to drink. That is the interesting thing about God in action. He delivers the miracle, but we have to play our part as well. Remember that you are a unique creation, not a robot. When God delivers, you have a role to play as well. He wants a relationship, not a race of empty-headed machines.

Prayer is a learned skill. It is not something that some people are gifted with and others aren't. It is like playing sports. You have to exercise the muscles, build up the endurance, and play the game every day to become any good at it. One of the most amazing things about being a Christian is that we not only have salvation and the promise of heaven, but Jesus places His Holy Spirit inside each of us. Just as Jesus walked and taught the disciples when He was on earth, the Holy Spirit works in each of our lives to bring us closer to Him. In Romans 8:26, Paul tells us that "the Spirit helps us in our weakness. We do not know what we ought to pray for, but the Spirit himself intercedes for us with groans that words cannot express. And he searches our hearts knows the mind of the Spirit because the Spirit intercedes for the saints in accordance with God's will." The Holy Spirit, inside every Christian actually can lead you where and what to pray for. Again, it comes from being in prayer, but you begin to develop to the ability to sense the leading of the Holy Spirit as he brings people and situations to your mind to pray for.

Prayer is worship. Above all, prayer is the acknowledgment that He is God, and we are not. That we are totally dependent upon Him! We worship Him by shouting out that He is our savior, our Creator, the source of our life, everything! Worship is a critical part of prayer. Forget the 'I want' lists, and start singing to Him. Psalm 100 says, "I will enter his courts with praise!" Can't figure out how to start praying? Start by telling God He is your every reason for being. The Bible says that God, "inhabits the praises of his people."

The more we worship, the more we realize the sin in our lives. When Isaiah came before God and saw the awesomeness of which God is, he cried out that he was "undone." The more we see God, the more we see our desperate need for God. The more we see that desperate need, the more we seek his forgiveness for who we are and the sins we continue to commit. The Bible says he is "faithful and just to forgive us." In Isaiah 66:2 it says he "rushes out to the aid of those who admit their desperate need for him." God wants us coming to Him. He can't wait to pour out his spirit on a person who loves to be with Him!

Worship Him with your prayers. Cry out your hurts, and your pains in prayer. Jerry Falwell used to always say, "Don't whine about it to other people, they can't do anything about it. Tell it to God, since he has the power to do something about your situation." Pray for each other. Samuel even considered it a sin when he forgot to pray: "Far be it from me that I should sin against the Lord by failing to pray for you." God's amazing plan for his people is built on a personal relationship with Him. Salvation comes from a personal, one-on-one acceptance of Jesus Christ as your savior. Your Christian life develops as you build a personal, one-on-one communication with God. He promises to "stick closer than a brother."

If you want to know God's will, pray. If you want to see God's destiny fulfilled in your life, pray. If you want to see your friends saved, pray. If you want to worship God, pray. If you want to see God active and powerful in your life, pray.

> If any of you lacks wisdom, he should ask God, who gives generously to all without finding fault, and it will be given to him. But when he asks, he must believe and not doubt, because he who doubts is like a wave of the sea, blown and tossed by the wind. That man should think he would not receive anything from the Lord; he is a double-minded man, unstable in all he does.
>
> —James 1:5–8 (NIV)

Real Prayer is intense. It is personal. Sometimes you will cry. Sometimes you will scream. The greatest prayer that I can think of in the Bible was the prayer Jesus made just before he was arrested. Look carefully at this prayer. It is anything but some meaningless dribble. It is specific, it is directed, and it is emotional! Jesus is laying it all out, and until we can open ourselves up in this way, our prayers will never get above the ceiling.

Read Matthew 17.

Now spend some real time in real prayer. Remember:

1. We learn to pray by praying
2. If we knew what God knows, we'd want what God wants!

Committed

Last October, in the wake of the shootings at Wedgewood Baptist Church, I received this email:

> By now almost everyone has heard of the tragedy that took place on September 15, when a gunman entered Wedgwood Baptist Church and killed 7 people and injured 7 others before taking his own life. That morning had been the day of "See You at the Pole," when students gather around their flagpole in the morning to pray for their school and nation. What the media hasn't reported, however, is how God has been so evident, both during and after the shooting. He has done amazing works!
>
> Before the Shooting:
>
> ***Our pastor, Brother Al, had prayed that God would do whatever it took to expand the ministry of Wedgwood Baptist Church. Our church is one that is used as a model of how NOT to pick a location, because no one in the world can find it. Now almost everyone in the world knows exactly where it is.
>
> Evidence of God's Control During the Shooting:
>
> ***To enter the church, the gunman walked past our children's playground, which should have been full of kids, but for some reason every single children's and preschool class was running late. No one had made it to the playground yet.
>
> ***He fired over 100 bullets into a crowd of over 400, but only 14 people were hit.
>
> ***He did not shoot the over 60 bullets he still had with him.
>
> ***The bottom fell off of the pipe bomb he threw, and then landed without ever exploding.
>
> ***One of the youths that was wounded (she was shielding a dis-

abled friend with her body) has scoliosis. The curve in her spine directed the bullet away from major organs, saving her from serious injury.
***Because the first 911 call came in on a police radio, emergency vehicles were dispatched immediately, without spending precious time to verify that the call was real.
***One of the people in the church at the time was a paramedic, and he was able to stop bleeding and stabilize injured people before the emergency crews arrived.
***Leaders were able to get the children out of the building without the kids having to see any victims or any of the mess.
***Each children's worker stayed with his/her class even though they all had children elsewhere in the building, and some had teens in the sanctuary. Not one worker left his or her post.
***None of the adults who died have children.
***All seven victims were not just Christians, but bold Christians who were passionate about their faith.
"You intended to harm me, but God intended it for good to accomplish what is not being done, the saving of many lives." (Genesis 50:20).

Or, what God has done since the shooting:
***Many denominations have pulled together to offer help and support. One example is the United Methodist Church who sent 15 people the following Sunday to cover our childcare. They didn't want any church members to have to miss the service because they were taking care of the children.
***A church in Tulsa, Oklahoma, drove over 5 hours just so they could march around our church and pray during our Sunday morning services.
***The Fort Worth Police Dept. planted flowers in the flowerbeds before we re-entered the sanctuary to worship.
***We have received over 10,000 emails, 5000 cards, and $60,000 from all over the world.
***Al Meredith, our pastor, has had the microphone in his face continually and has over and over given an outstanding answer to the reason for our hope.

He presented the gospel beautifully on *Larry King Live*, when prompted by a question asked by Vice President Al Gore.

***Because of the live news coverage and interviews, over 200 million people have heard the gospel because of this tragedy.

***Fifteen thousand turned out for a community-wide service at TCU football stadium. Brother Al gave a very serious, challenging message calling for a day of fasting and heart searching (Monday the 20th). The service was broadcast live in its entirety on WBAP 820, which is a news station that covers most of north Texas. This same news station has replayed our pastor's first press conference due to people calling in and requesting to hear his comforting words again.

***CNN also broadcast the memorial service live. Amazingly, because one of the victim's families lives and works in Saudi Arabia, that country allowed the service to be broadcast there as well. In Saudi Arabia it is illegal to say the name of Jesus on the street.

***Because of that same CNN broadcast, 35 people in Japan gave their lives to Christ.

***When President Clinton finally got through to him, Brother Al ended their conversation by praying, after gaining permission, for the Clinton family.

***At several schools, students met around their flagpoles the next day. At one school 25 students accepted Christ, and 110 at another.

***A teacher led 22 students to Christ in her classroom.

***Christian teachers all over North Texas have been able to share with their classes because the students are asking questions about their teachers' faith.

***In Burleson, prayers and Scripture are being said over the intercom.

***On the East Coast, where "See You at the Pole" was delayed because of the hurricane, record numbers of kids showed up to pray

***Governor Bush and the Fort Worth mayor quietly came to our pastor's home while the staff were meeting and praying and joined in the prayer meeting.

This was not political! Only those who are close to staff members heard about this; the media never knew.
***Governor Bush has visited with our pastor several times, and Brother Al has had an impact on him. Just think of the influence that our pastor could have if Governor Bush is the next president!
***A caller to an area Christian radio station said that he didn't know what those people had but he wanted it. The DJ proceeded to lead him to Christ.

Many notes left in front of the church contain the same sentiment. Those who don't know Jesus want what we have!
***The church has received so many emails asking us how we are able to have hope and continue on. There are teams of church member volunteers responding to these emails.
***My friend Jodi has been praying for her husband for years. She and their 4-yr-old daughter were at the church that night. Three days ago, Scott gave his life to Christ.
***We have had over 70,000 hits on our web page, which displays the plan of salvation in multiple languages.
***Many members at Wedgwood Baptist are healing broken relationships within the body and experiencing spiritual renewal.

These are just a few of the miracles that are happening. God's grace is almost overwhelming. Every time the gunman fired a bullet, he intended to take a life. Yet God turned that around and saved several lives for each bullet fired. The faith of those who died has been multiplied many times over. "I thank my God through Jesus Christ for all of you, because your faith is being reported all over the world." (Romans 1:8).

Columbine, Wedgewood, Heath High School in Paducah: these are not isolated, random incidents. God is at work to show Himself to a generation that has been brought to the "kingdom for such a time as this." Did God cause all of this misery to happen? No, but He did work and move through the situation to accomplish His will. The Bible says "all things work together for good." So often, though, it takes a tragedy to get us to stop living for ourselves, and see the world as God sees it. These are desperate times.

Your friends are living in a generation that is in danger of losing all connection to a God that loves them. The only thing standing in the way is you. "In 1992, a *USA Weekend* survey of over 236,000 young people revealed that 25 to 40 percent of teens see nothing wrong with cheating on exams, stealing from employers, or keeping money that isn't theirs." (Tribe, p. 99) Worse than that,

> In a time when society lacks clear ethical guidelines, when parents neither spend the time to educate about time-honored values such as honesty, integrity, and personal responsibility nor necessarily model consistent values in their own lives, kids are responding to the one message they hear loud and strong from the adult world: succeed. Do well. Do whatever you need to *do*.
>
> —(Tribe, p. 99)

The reason the message that there is right, there is wrong, and there is a God who loves them, is not being heard is because we aren't shouting it out. We have become so apathetic and cynical in our lives that we have allowed the world's way to become acceptable. The church is a weak, ineffective reflection of the church Christ called us to be. It is time we stop being timid. It is time we stop being silent. It is time we stand up and start showing a gray world that there is black and white. It is up to you. You and I can't wait for our youth pastor, our church, or our friends to take the lead. Jesus has already given us the command: go. In this day and age, churches all over America are Christian in name only, and in fact, have shut Jesus out of His own church.

Rick Ferguson, pastor of Riverside Baptist Church in Denver, said that "We have become so self-absorbed, so self-sufficient, so self-confident, and so self-focused that one day Jesus didn't show up for church, and nobody noticed He was gone." This is the view I see of many youth groups in this country. We are so focused on ski trips, pizza parties, and lock-ins that we haven't bothered to witness, worship or pray. Jesus has left the building, and nobody even noticed. In the Book of Revelation, Jesus delivers a message to a church very much like most of us in America. It is a frightening wake-up call, and if we are going to see God's destiny in our lives, we had better listen up. The church that Jesus is talking to in Revelation chapter 3 is in a place called Laodicea. In verse 20, we see Jesus knocking on the door of this church, wanting to come in and spend time with his church. The problem is this: nobody hears him knocking. Inside, the church is so content with their activities and their busy lives that they don't care that Jesus is locked out of his own church. Do we?

The city of Laodicea was a wealthy city. They were the center of banking and trade. They had a huge gold reserve, and they produced many unique products that weren't available anywhere else in the world. They were a center of fashion, as well. This was the New York City of their day. The people there were living the good life. They had the best of everything and lived their lives as they wanted. God, however, saw them as desperate, lost, and in serious trouble. They had such a bloated, inflated opinion of themselves, that they couldn't even see how pathetic they really were.

Jesus is bringing them, and us, quite a wake-up call in Revelation 3. He has had enough of a church that is bored and tired. We know the creator of the universe, personally! We have a God who handcrafted each of us! We have a Lord who has a unique plan for our lives! How can church be boring? How can we come to church, and be "unemotional?" How can we be connected to a loving, living God and not get excited? Jesus himself WANTS to come into our lives and stands at the door knocking. How can we keep Him outside? Yet that is exactly what the church in Laodicea was doing. They had become casual, uninterested, and bored with church life. A living, vibrant church, had become a dull, lifeless country club. Jesus says in Revelation 3:15 that "I know your deeds. Yet because you are lukewarm, neither hot nor cold, I am going to vomit you out of my mouth." Get the picture? Not spit; vomit. This lukewarm attitude is so disgusting to God that he vomits. Not to get gross here, but you know what happens when you throw up. Your whole body convulses to get whatever is in, out. Your body will do nothing else till it gets rid of what it doesn't want. When we just exist, we do that to Jesus. Casual Christianity is not Christianity at all. It makes Christ sick! We can't live it both ways. He is either Lord of all, or not at all.

Remember, Jesus said in the first part of the verse, "I know your deeds" and it doesn't make any difference. He knows how many times we have gone to church. He knows how many mission trips we went on, how many times we read our Bible, and how much money we have put in the offering plate, and He doesn't care. Why? We have done it with a wrong motive. Jesus doesn't want to be a part of our life; he wants to be our whole life! You don't fit the kind of relationship with Jesus that changes a world into your life. It must be your life! How would you feel if you had given your blood to rescue a friend who won't even bother to open the door for you? That is exactly the message Christ is giving to a people who have decided they don't really need Him around. Who are you? Are you passionate for Jesus? Does He fill every moment of your life? Or is He something you do on Sunday, get your fix for the week, and carry on the rest of the time with or without Him. It is time we got radical. It is time we got red-hot! It is time we start sharing the love of Christ in every moment of our lives!

One of the greatest dangers facing the average American church today, is the danger of "self-confidence" and "self-sufficiency." If we place our confidence in anything else other than the Lord Jesus Christ. . . . we are in desperate trouble.

- Churches can place their confidence in their programs and procedures
- Churches can place their confidence in their traditions

- Churches can place their confidence in their own plans and strategies
- Churches can place their confidence in their finances and when they do. . . . They are on a sure road to self-destruction.

—Dr. Rick Ferguson, Riverside Baptist Church

If this world is going to change, then this generation must come to a place where we place our dependence, our confidence, our hope, our future, and our very lives in the hands of Jesus Christ. Hebrews 11:6 says, "Without faith, you cannot please God." This is the church of America! In a world where 80 percent of Christians in America have NEVER shared their faith, we don't need much more evidence to realize WE are lukewarm. It doesn't matter what others think of you, it doesn't matter what you think of yourself, what really matter is what God thinks of you. Your self-image, your purpose, everything you are comes from a vibrant, real relationship with Jesus Christ. Anything else is lulling you into a mind-numbing existence, and that is no destiny.

Jesus loves us too much, though, to leave us in that state. He wants us to be on fire for him. He doesn't want us to just get by. He wants us to achieve all that He has planned for our lives. So, he keeps knocking on the door. He says in verse 19 that "Those whom I love, I reprove and discipline; be zealous, therefore, and repent." Repentance is one of those big, "churchly" words that we hear a great deal about. Repentance is the first step to becoming a Christian, and it is repentance that keeps us developing in our lives with Christ. It simply means realizing you've done something wrong, changing course, and saying you are sorry. When we repent, we not only ask forgiveness, we make a definite change of course and leave sin behind.

Finding that freedom keeps our hearts zealous and excited. This is the only relationship that can give your life true meaning. We try to fill the void of God with everything else, and it all leaves us empty. Teenagers search and look into everything to a reason for living. Why am I here? What should I do with my life? We try everything to fill that sense of eternity. We get into New Age philosophy, we believe in our horoscopes, we watch the skies for alien visitors, we place our hopes and dreams on becoming like that face on the television, or that voice on the radio. We try everything imaginable to fill that sense of purpose, and when we can't fill it, we hide from it through drugs, alcohol, sex, and any number of other diversions. But only ONE thing can give us a sense of peace and purpose: a personal, gut-level, intimate relationship with the Son of the LIVING God in the person of Jesus Chirst. I'm not just talking about accepting Jesus and becoming a Christian. I'm talking about the next step as well: falling so deeply in love with Him that the world fades away and your vision becomes clear. Your destiny is right in front of you. Jeremiah called it a "fire shut up in my bones" that he couldn't hold inside. That is a fire that can change the world.

Then we must accept the responsibility for our world. In a world that is hanging on the edge, we cannot sit by and play our church games. We have to be active, vocal, and unwavering in the truth of the Gospel. We, as Christians, serve a living, powerful, almighty, holy, perfect God. Yet we act as if we were the children of a failure. Wake up! Arise! Stop hiding in your hallways and keeping your church life on a shelf until Sunday morning. God created your inmost being, He is all of you, in you, and wrapped around you. If you have Jesus Christ in your heart, then hold to the promise that "I can do ALL things through Christ who strengthens me." It is time to stop being afraid. It is time to give up our pathetic excuses for prayer and start calling down the power of God into our lives. It is time that youth groups, and especially youth ministers, start blowing off the pizza parties and start having anointed, powerful prayer for the teenage missionaries of their church who are going to walk onto their mission field Monday morning.

The world tells us that teenagers won't respond to God, that the Bible is irrelevant. In our "enlightened" age, we have no need for talk of sin. The news media tells us that witnessing, and evangelism is "manipulative," and even "cult-like." Teenagers are a media-driven generation, raised on video games and MTV. They have no use for Jesus. That is a lie straight from the pits of a very real hell. This generation is desperate for something concrete and committed. A reason, and a hope that is worth living for. They have watched their families fall apart. They have seen their political leaders lie, cheat, and steal. They have been taught that there is no right, there is no wrong, and "whatever works for you" is the way to life.

Christian teenager, your entire life and being should be flying in the face of that "world-view." There is right, there is wrong. There is a Savior. There is only one way to know God. There is only one way to heaven. The reality of a life with Christ hasn't gone out of style; it has just been swept under the rug and hidden from a people desperate to fill their God-given sense of eternity and purpose.

> In many ways it is the departure of the Church from preaching that is responsible in a large measure for the state of modern society. . . . The Church, having abandoned her real task, has left humanity more or less to its own devices.
>
> —Martyn Lloyd-Jones

Why does it take a horrific act like Columbine to wake us up? We have become so complacent, so comfortable, so lazy, and so inactive, that we have become the Laodociean Church. A church that is so pathetic and useless that is makes God sick to the point of wanting to vomit.

Teenager, youth leader, and pastor, whomever you are: turn the tide. The church can only be the church when it exists out in the world. If we have a passion for Christ, then we cannot hide behind our walls, and our comfortable pews any longer. It is passion that drives us to shout out the truth of Christ. Is it easy? No. The truth of Christ is not tolerant, it is not politically correct, it is not pretty. But, it is truth.

Timothy was a young pastor when he received the letters from Paul that make up the books of 1 and 2 Timothy. In it, Paul says it very plainly to every one of us: "Do the work of an evangelist." "Preach the word." "Be strong." John MacArthur Jr., in his book, *Ashamed of the Gospel,* said this: "We have nothing else worth saying. There is no other message. There is no other valid ministry." I don't want to be, or be a part of a church that is disgusting to God. Lukewarm, casual, ineffective Christianity is not Christianity at all. It is living a lie.

In verse 21 of Revelation, however, Jesus gives us the hope of answering His knock at our door: "To him who overcomes, I will grant to him to sit down with Me on My throne, as I also overcame and sat down with My Father on His throne." Jesus would have not have made the promise to you of being an "overcomer" if were not possible to be an "overcomer." No matter what your situation, you can overcome it. No matter what the hardship, you can overcome it. God created you to be a winner. You can be an overcomer in a home where you are the only Christian. You can be an overcomer in that hell you walk through every day at school. You can be an overcomer in a lukewarm youth group. You can be an overcomer in a dead church. If you are not living an overcoming life, then it is because you are not doing it. As we have discussed, God has given you every resource you need to accomplish His will for you from before you were born. He has promised to his people that He would never leave us nor forsake us. His word tells us that "All things are possible," and that if "God is for us, who can be against us." Now, either we believe our Savior, hold onto him, and follow him as overcomers, or we are lukewarm, casual Christians, living a pathetic excuse for a Godly life. Jesus says, "Take heart, because I have overcome the world."

There is nothing you can go through that Jesus hasn't dealt with and overcome, and because He has victory, we have victory through Him! Stop believing in this Jerry Springer mentality of life that says you are a victim. Everything in your life is not someone else's fault; it is yours. Stop making every sin into some sort of condition or disease that allows you to pass the blame. The genetic tendency for alcoholism is very much a part of your genetic makeup, but becoming a drunk is your choice. In Romans 8:37, it says that we are "more than conquerors through Christ." If the Holy Spirit is alive, well, and breathing inside of you, then don't you dare call yourself a victim. Through a vital relationship with Christ you are a victor, not a victim. You only become a victim of your own sin when you step outside of God's will for your life.

The Bible says that if any man is "in Christ," he is a "new creation." That creation is not a victim, he is not lukewarm, and he is not casual about his faith. If we are "in Christ," then we have his power at work in our lives!

> 35 Who shall separate us from the love of Christ? Shall tribula-
> tion, or distress, or persecution, or famine, or nakedness, or peril,
> or sword?
> 36 Just as it is written, "For Thy sake we are being put to death all
> day long; we were considered as sheep to be slaughtered."
> 37 But in all these things we overwhelmingly conquer through
> Him who loved us.
> 38 For I am convinced that neither death, nor life, nor angels, nor
> principalities, nor things present, nor things to come, nor powers,
> 39 nor height, nor depth, nor any other created thing, shall be
> able to separate us from the love of God, which is in Christ Jesus
> our Lord.
>
> —Romans 8: (New American Standard)

Don't give up, don't quit, and don't ever become casual about your faith. God has birthed in you a destiny, now it is up to us to do the work. We can only accomplish great things when we stayed close and sensitive to God's work in our lives. When God chose Solomon to build the temple in the Old Testament, he told him, "I have chosen you to build this temple, now be strong and do the work." We have a duty to perform. We have to be overcomers in this life. We have to do the work God calls us to do. We have to seek out a relationship with Him that grows deeper each day. Then we will remain hot for His presence in our lives and never become a disgusting, lukewarm, casual Christian.

> 16 For the Lord himself shall descend from heaven with a shout, with the voice of the archangel, and with the trump of God: and the dead in Christ shall rise first:
> 17 Then we, which are alive and remain, shall be caught up together with them in the clouds, to meet the Lord in the air: and so shall we ever be with the Lord.
>
> —1 Thess 4: (King James)

Fulfilling the Destiny of Commitment

Setting the spark . . . Most people in this world are spectators. We dream of being the big star, the super athlete, or the powerful political leader. In truth, however, most of us are content to just be the dreamers. We often feel that God has plans for other people, but not us. Wrong! God has the plan. The question is; do we have the commitment? When Moses' time of leadership was done, God chose a young man named Joshua to take up the call and lead the enormous population of Israel into the land that God had promised them.
Read Joshua 1: 1–9.

1. What advice did God give Joshua three times in these first nine verses?

2. The Lord told Joshua not be terrified, and not to be afraid . . . why?

____

3. According to the Lord in verse 8, what is the key to prosperity and success?

____

Fanning the flame . . . It is interesting that God tells Joshua in the first verse that "Moses is dead." Joshua had been mourning the death of Moses for several weeks, so this was not any news flash to him. Why did God tell him that? To remind him that Moses is gone. Moses fulfilled the destiny in his life; now I have a new destiny for you, Joshua. God is not limited by time or by man. He will always have a Moses or a Joshua for the time and place that he has called them to. Moses is dead. Now it is your turn. This is your time.

Read Exodus 3:10–17

1. What did God ask Moses to do?

____

2. What was the response of Moses?

____

3. What reason did God give as an answer to Moses' excuses?

____

Moses is one of the most powerful figures in the Bible. Yet, time and time again, Moses tries to "chicken out" of doing what God is telling him to do.

Read Exodus 4:13.

Moses' excuse is no different from the ones we use today. Truth be known, most of us like our lives on the sidelines, but that is not the destiny of God for you. Nobody is called to sit on the bench. God has a position for all of us to play, and He becomes angry when we want someone else to do the job that He created us to do.

Read all of Exodus 4.

List three excuses that you have used for not doing what you know God wants you to do.

1. ______________________________
2. ______________________________
3. ______________________________

Igniting the passion . . . Paul was not one to put up with excuses. He often attacked the kind of pathetic, "side-line" Christianity. God has called us to be winners. He has called us to be overcomers.

Read Romans 8:28–39

Commit to read this passage of Scripture every day during your quiet time. After reading it, pray that God would show you areas in your life when you have been a spectator, when God wants you on the field. Write them down here, and make the commitment to be more than a conqueror.

1. ______________________________
2. ______________________________
3. ______________________________

Connected

If you asked me to sum up my life in one word, it would have to be "friendships." It starts when you are young, learning to play with the kids in the neighborhood. I remember the softball games that would stretch into dusk on a summer night. Bicycle trips to the dreaded end of the street, where you didn't dare go any farther into the unknown world that lay on the next corner. We would spend our days exploring the "wilderness" of the small creek that ran through our neighborhood. Those woods could become anything: a war-torn country, a castle court, or some post-nuclear war town. It didn't matter what we were all doing, the point is, we were together. When you hit junior high, it is all about whose mom can take you to the mall and who is going to pick you up. Once there, the world is yours. You are an independent adult in the world of the mall. You can do whatever you want, hang with your friends, and be seen by everyone. Dating also becomes the priority. You have no idea what to do on a date, and you are scared to death, but you manage to play it cool. In high school, the need for your friends becomes more intense. The world becomes not-so-perfect, and you start dealing with serious issues. Throughout my high school years, my friends and I walked each other through issues over alcohol, drugs, suicide, guns in the school, violence, and death. God designed us to be in relationships. Part of his plan is for us to have these kind of deep relationships with people.

It is not good for man to be alone. I will make a helper suitable for

> him. Now the Lord God had formed out of the ground all the beasts of the field and all the birds of the air. He brought them to the man to see what he would name them; and whatever the man called each living creature, that was its name. So the man gave names to all the livestock, the birds of the air and all the beasts of the field. But for Adam, no suitable helper was found. So the Lord God caused the man to fall into a deep sleep: and while he was sleeping he took one of the man's ribs and closed up the place with flesh. Then the Lord God made a woman from the rib of the man, and he brought her to the man. The man said, "This is now bone of my bones and flesh of my flesh; she shall be called 'woman,' for she was taken out of man."
>
> —Genesis 1:18–23 (NIV)

When God designed you, he put into you a mechanism that causes you to have a need for relationships. We need our friends, our families, a lifelong mate, and deep intimate relationships throughout every stage of our life. The problem is, people get hurt and wounded at places in their life due to sin, and improper relationships. As a result, they become "gun-shy" about getting into a new relationship. "I won't get hurt again," and fears of being cut that deep hold us back from opening ourselves up the next time. Our present relationships are based on our past relationships. People protect and hold themselves in. As a result, they place themselves in their own bondage. God made you to experience life. He made you to know love. First and foremost, His love, but also the love of other people.

Often, it is the church that can do the worst damage. Jesus is the perfect head of the church, but we are the body. We, as a people who are supposed to be known by our love, are oftentimes as bad as, if not worse than the world. We, as a church, can destroy people without even realizing we are doing it. Why? God will equip and strengthen you, yes. But we have to do our part in his kingdom as well. He will only help us in our relationships as we help ourselves. Relationships involve you! To have a friend, you have to be a friend. You have to make a conscious effort to develop and keep real relationships. Will that solve everything? Will you not ever get hurt again? No, people will always let you down. The point is to get up and keep working at a relationship. We let Jesus down on a minute-to-minute basis, over and over again. Yet, He never gives up on us. He promises to "never leave us or forsake us." What right do we have to turn away if a friend hurts us? The church can be broken, destroyed, and made ineffective in the world, not by forces from the outside, but by the destructive forces from within. When we let hurt feelings, wounds, and baggage from our past, simmer and burn in us, we give the devil a destructive foothold.

I grew up in a great church. I am so grateful that those early years were spent with great friendships, a deep love of God, and some excellent examples of Christian life. However, when I was sixteen, problems began to develop. A disagreement among the staff was slowly spilling over into the congregation. To this day, I have no idea what happened, but little by little, lines were drawn and families took sides. Close family relationships fell apart, and God left the church. The lost were not important. God was not important. Worship was nonexistent. All that mattered was whose side you were on. One by one, the entire staff left. A deacon had a physical confrontation with the pastor, and the church fell apart. Finally, the church split in half. The results of that senseless, useless battle are obvious. The youth group that finished its tenure before "the split," spawned five pastors, with several others in active ministry work to this day. Most of those teens are still active in church today.

My youth group, however, had a far different result. Most are not active in any church today. Their children are growing up without God. Most became involved in drinking and the party scene. Just because you find problems with people in the church does not mean that the church is full of hypocrites and liars! It means that we are human, failed, flawed, sinful people who are working day by day to become more like Jesus and sometimes we miss the mark. The point is you don't quit. You turn around and head right after Jesus again! There are no perfect friends. There are no perfect families. There are no perfect relationships. If you put that responsibility on someone, you will be let down time and time again. You will fail in any relationship if you cannot accept imperfections. Only Christ and His relationship with us are a perfect relationship. Even our relationship to Him is often flawed. That is why a wedding vow is about "for better or worse." A relationship is about hard work, commitment, and not giving up on someone. I have met so many people who are "church jumpers." They join a church and talk about how great everyone is, how wonderful everyone is. After about five years, they are leaving because they don't feel there is any "love" in the church. Then they repeat the process all over again. The problem is not that the people in the church changed, it is just that you got to know them! You found out that they are not perfect! The active, reaching body of Christ is about working through the problems, dealing with issues, committing to each other, and moving on for Christ!

When we isolate ourselves from people, we are opening ourselves up to failure. We must have accountability. We must be active in godly relationships, or we will fall. In 1 Kings 19, we see that Elijah sends his only friend away from him. Elijah was scared and on the run. He had done all of these amazing things, but now he figures his life is over. So what does he do? He cuts himself off from everyone who cares about him. He goes into the desert and begs God to kill him. Depression, hopelessness, and defeat thrive on loneliness.

We are created to be in active, productive relationships with other people! When God was in the garden of Eden, he decided that it "is not good for man to be alone." He saw that part of our makeup was the need to be with other people! Why? We are made in the image of God. God wanted to have a relationship with us, so it only makes sense that a part of us has a need to have relationships with Him, and with each other.

It is a proven fact that you cannot stand on your own. Proverbs says that if you "walk WITH the wise, you will grow wise." Quality relationships, with godly people, are the key to fulfilling your destiny in this life! Without Christian people speaking truth, holding you accountable, picking you up when you fall, and holding on to you, you will not succeed. Even Jesus saw the importance of friendships. One of his first actions in his ministry years was to recruit the disciples, and they never left his side. Quality friendships, with fellow believers, are critical to your survival!

However, we should never try to get from our relationships what we can only get from an active relationship with Jesus Christ. God is our only source of identity, self-worth, and value. Disassociate your sense of value from your friends. Your worth in this world is based on Jesus Christ. It is never based on your friends, your boyfriend or girlfriend, or the people who you hang around with. A real friendship should be a source of strength and encouragement. It should never be your identity. Remember that God has a plan for your life. He has relationships—a wife or husband—and the quality influences you need already in your path. Don't waste your time on a relationship that pulls you down, or makes you think you are nothing without that person. You are a unique creation of the Lord, God Almighty. Don't give a destructive relationship access to your destiny. It is just not worth it.

> There was a man all alone; he had neither son nor brother. There was no end to his toil, yet his eyes were not content with his wealth. "For whom am I toiling," he asked, "and why am I depriving myself of enjoyment?" This too is meaningless—a miserable business! Two are better than one, because they have a good return for their work: if one falls down, his friend can help him up. But pity the man who falls and has no one to help him up!
>
> —Ecclesiastes 4:8–11 (NIV)

We all get down sometimes. Everyone has those times when we feel defeated. If we are alone, we are open to the attacks of the devil. He can convince us we are worthless and hopeless. But when you have support, you have people around you that will hold you up and keep you going in the hard times.

> They took an oath to the Lord, with loud acclamation, with shouting and with trumpets and horns. All Judah rejoiced about the oath because they had sworn it wholeheartedly. They sought God eagerly, and he was found by them. So the Lord gave them rest on every side.
>
> —2 Chronicles 15:13,14 (NIV)

The Israelites, as a connected group, made an oath to follow God. The Bible says they made sacrifices and committed to God, wholeheartedly.

That's the key to building a ministry. Commit yourself to God. Commit yourselves as a unit to God, and be willing to make the sacrifice to follow him. These kinds of relationships are called "covenant" relationships. It is not "hanging around" kind of friendships that develop your relationship with God. Those are acquaintances. Real friends, covenant relationships, require commitment, time, energy, laughter as well as tears, prayer, and accountability to each other. Proverbs 18:24 says, "The man who is a friend of all the world will prove himself a friend to none, but there is a friend who sticks closer than a brother." Committed relationships, either in a marriage, a family, or a friendship, produce a covenant. Covenant relationships bring about security, strength, and encouragement. Only a covenant relationship can help us on our walk to fulfill our destiny.

Intimacy, however, is costly. An intimate relationship with Christ and intimate relationships with other people can be scary. They demand us to offer our time, our emotions, to make sacrifices, and sometimes we can get wounded. Without them, the cost is much greater. God never intends for us to be alone in our journey.

> The harvest is plentiful but the workers are few. Ask the Lord of the Harvest, therefore, to send out workers into his harvest field.
>
> —Matthew 9: 37–38 (NIV)

God is building a team of individuals. We are unique, we are special, and we are complete in Christ. We don't need any other relationship than Christ to be complete. However, part of God's design is that we are active in relationships that encourage us, hold us together, and point us to Jesus. That is true of our dating relationships, our families, and our friendships. Relationships take time, commitment, and sacrifice. But, quality friendships, committed families, and pure dating relationships can lead us closer to Jesus and closer to fulfilling our destiny in this world.

> Jonathan said to David, "Go in peace, for we have sworn friendship with each other in the name of the Lord, saying, 'The Lord is witness between you and me, and between your descendants and my descendants forever.' "
>
> And Jonathan had David reaffirm his oath out of love for him, because he loved him as he loved himself.
>
> —1 Samuel 20: 16, 42 (NIV)

Fulfilling the Destiny of Friendship

Setting the spark . . . Being alone is something that we are simply not designed for. God's perfect plan always has us involved with people. In the Garden of Eden, God decided that Adam shouldn't be alone, and He created Eve. Jesus didn't spend his ministry years on earth alone, he chose twelve men who would share the work and be companions to Jesus. God designed the unique experience of marriage and family so that we would always be connected to other people in love. Being alone gives birth to depression, hurt, and sin. When we feel like we are alone, we start looking for other things to fill the hole left by loneliness. Often, that leads to poor substitutes such as drugs, alcohol, and sex outside of its intended place in marriage.

Read Acts 12: 1–19

1. Peter was arrested and kept in prison. What had happened to his friend James and would likely happen to him?

   ____

2. What were Peter's friends doing while he was in prison?

   ____

3. Where did Peter go, as soon as he realized that he was free from prison?

   ____

Fanning the flame . . . Peter had committed friends. The entire time that he was held, his friends kept praying "earnestly" for him. They didn't stop. They prayed for him day after day, and night after night. Committed friendships are the key to the work of the Lord. That is why the church is so important! It is part of God's plan that we are connected to a group of people who stick with us through thick and thin. You should never just come in the door, sit down, put in your time, and leave.

Read Hebrews 10: 24, 25

What are the three things God commands us to do in our friendships?

1. ______________________________
2. ______________________________
3. ______________________________

Read Ephesians 4:30–32

We need to love people the way Christ loves us. If Christ can forgive us, we must be willing to forgive others when they hurt us. We have to put aside our anger, our fear, and our hatred. It is an old saying, but it is still true: if you want a friend, you have to be a friend. Our strongest loyalties in life should be to God, our families, and our friends. In fact, most of the problems in our society today come from a breakdown of commitment to the family and our friends. Why would a kid join a gang? Because he is desperate to feel like he belongs to a group; that he is not alone. If the family is gone, and committed friendships are gone, where else could he turn but to some counterfeit for love, created by the world?

Igniting a passion . . . Paul understood the need for committed relationships. He speaks often of it in his letters to the churches. Though he speaks on marriages, friendships, and church relationships, he sums it all up in one amazing chapter.

Read Romans 12.

List three friends with whom you need to rebuild your relationship this week. Take the time to call them, write to them, or visit with them. Spend twenty minutes in prayer for each of them, and your relationship with them. Apologize for the wounds you may have caused, or forgive them for the hurt they may have caused you. Get your friendships and your family relationships back on track. Holding on to bitterness or wounds from your past just creates baggage that will continue to drag you down from achieving the destiny that God has designed for you.

1. ______________________________
2. ______________________________
3. ______________________________

Worshiper

I doubt that for as long as I live, I shall never forget a Monday night in June that changed my life. I had gone to a worship service at a camp not expecting a whole lot. The band was great, the crowd was lively, but I didn't think there was anything to special going on. The band, Nobleman's Son, began a song called "Thunder in the Desert." I thought it was a nice touch that they had the sound of rolling thunder as part of the song . . . only, it wasn't a sound effect.

Outside, a storm had rolled in. Thunder and lightning were crashing all around the auditorium. The seven hundred students inside carried on with the service. Suddenly, an enormous crash of lightning and thunder plunged the whole auditorium into darkness. Just then, one of the emergency doors gave way, and a river of water poured into the auditorium. In the darkness, as water flowed everywhere, you could hear singing out to God like I have never heard. Despite the darkness, despite the water, everyone in the room was crying out to God with an unquenchable passion. When the lights came back, hardly anyone was standing. Most were on their knees, tears streaming down their face, as they cried out to a Lord they dearly loved. So often, we talk about the "power of God," but when you come face to face with it, it is easy to see why Moses' face was radiant after coming down from being with God on Mount Sinai. I have often heard people say things like, "When I get to heaven, I want to tell God this," or "I want to know why He let this happen." After an experience like that, I can tell you this much: when we see God, we will be able to do nothing but fall on our knees and praise Him with all we've got. John MacArthur Jr. called worship our "ultimate priority." Throughout the Bible, God stresses the importance, indeed the necessity of, worship.

In the Bible we find that Israel had a king who knew how to worship the Lord. He knew how to "love the Lord with all his heart, with all his soul, and with all his mind." His name was David, and the story of his life *began* with killing Goliath, it didn't end there. David was the greatest king in Israel's history. He could not be stopped in battle, his country had the best economy of any in the known world, he was a hero, and he is the only person in the Bible that God calls a "man after my own heart." He knew God's heart, because he made worship his ultimate priority. He knew God's heart, because he realized that his strength came from being on his knees before his God. Here is a man who had it all . . . dozens of children, wealth, many wives, success, power, honor, anything he could want. But David wasn't concerned about any of the world's charms. He wanted God:

> One thing I ask of the Lord, this is what I seek: that I may dwell in the house of the Lord all the days of my life, to gaze upon the beauty of the Lord and to seek Him in his temple.
>
> —Psalm 27:4 (NIV)

David wanted three things, and they are the three things we should value most: to dwell in the house of the Lord, to gaze upon the beauty of the Lord, and to seek Him in his temple. Let's look at the first one: to dwell in the house of the Lord. What is the house of the Lord?

> Blessed are those who dwell in your house; they are ever praising you.
>
> —Psalm 84:4 (NIV)

We can't even praise the Lord for twenty minutes on a Sunday morning without getting distracted and worrying about what everyone around us might think if we lift our hands. But the Bible says that if we are in the Lord's house, we are "ever praising you." Ephesians 3:17 says, "so that Christ may dwell in your hearts through faith."If you want to dwell in the house of the Lord you need look no further than your own heart. Are you ever praising him? Or are you too busy destroying the house of the Lord that you can't even see Jesus inside you, let alone praise the one who gave you life. Psalm 34:5 says that "Those who look to him are RADIANT!" In Psalm 34:1, David says clearly "His praise will always be on my lips!" It is time to clean up the house of the Lord. It is time to bring your life into worship. It is time for us to meet Jesus face to face in our lives. Do you think the world has something better? Do we really think that the drugs, the sex, the alcohol, the parties, the popularity, the girlfriends will fill our lives? Is being devoted to Jesus going to cost you too much? Could it be that there a part of you that still thinks the world still has something that Jesus can't give you? Look at David. He had everything. "If I can get a car, then everything will be all right." David had an entire army to take him anywhere he wanted to go. Do you have a girlfriend or boyfriend? David had a dozen wives. He has got us beat on wealth, fame, anything you can come up with, but here is where it counts:

> Better is one day in your courts than a thousand elsewhere; I would rather be a doorkeeper in the house of my God than dwell in the tents of the wicked.
>
> —Psalm 84:10

David had it all, and none of it mattered. Being with God, worshiping God is all he wanted to do. A. W. Tozer said that he would rather "worship God than do anything else in the entire world." Do you know what it means to worship like that? Do you know what it means to be so lost in telling God you love him that you lose all track of time? Do you know what it means to sing to the Lord with tears streaming down your face because you love Him so much? If you don't, then you don't even know what it means to be a Christian. You have missed the biggest part of the Christian life. If being a Christian involves following Jesus, and Jesus' greatest commandment is to love the Lord with all your heart, and your heart is where the Lord dwells, then it's time we had our hearts broken before God. It's time we tell our Savior we love Him more than anything. If you have spent any amount of time in church, then you have sung countless praise chorus and hymns, but do you believe and take to heart the words behind those songs?

Next, David says he wants to gaze upon the beauty of the Lord. First Peter 3:3 says this of the Lord's beauty:

> Your beauty should not come from outward adornments, such as braided hair and the wearing of gold jewelry and fine clothes. Instead, it should be that of your inner self, the unfading beauty of a gentle and quiet spirit, which is of great worth in God's sight.

If the Lord dwells in our heart, then we should reflect his beauty: the unfading beauty of a gentle and quiet spirit. Have you ever seen anyone who has met God face to face? You can see it in their eyes. People who are worshipers have this glow about them, and I love to look in their eyes, because they are blazing with the light of God. You can see it coming right up out of their souls. These are people who worship. These are people who praise the Lord. Tozer describes it this way:

> God desires to take us deeper into Himself. We will have much to learn in the school of the spirit. He wants to lead us on in our love for Him who first loved us. He wants to cultivate within us the adoration and admiration of which He is worthy. He wants to reveal to each of us the blessed element of spiritual fascination in true

worship. He wants to teach us the wonder of being filled with moral excitement in our worship, entranced with the knowledge of who God is. He wants us to be astonished at the elevation and magnitude and splendor of Almighty God! There can be no substitute for this kind of worship and for this kind of spirit-given response to the God who is our Creator and Redeemer and Lord!

Is He worth it to you? He is your creator. Psalm 139 says he "knit us together in our mother's womb." He is your redeemer. He sent His only son into this world to set us free from the destruction the world would give us. If you really believe that, then you better be willing to live it. You had better be willing to shout about it, you had better be willing to "shout to the Lord all the earth let us sing." He has set you free from sin, free from bondage, free from drugs, free from failure, free from low self-esteem, free from your past, and the Bible says that "whom the son sets free, is free indeed!" If that doesn't set your eyes ablaze, get your heart pumping, and send your heart soaring, then you better see if you ever even have met Jesus in the first place! Gaze upon the beauty of the Lord. Look what has happened to everyone in the Bible who have seen God face to face:

Jacob sees him one night and thanks the Lord that he lived. We turn his name into a curse word and don't even think twice about it. In Exodus 34:29, Moses came down from the mountain after meeting God carrying the Ten Commandments and the Bible says that "*He was not aware that his face was radiant because he had spoken with the Lord.*"

In 2 Corinthians 3:18, it says that "*And we, who with unveiled faces all reflect the Lord's glory, are being transformed into his likeness with ever-increasing glory, which comes from the Lord, who is the spirit.*"

It doesn't stop there: look at Matthew 17:2, the disciples see Jesus. "*His face shone like the sun, and his clothes became as white as light.*"

Go on to Acts 6:15: "*All that were sitting in the Sanhedrin looked intently at Stephen, and they saw that his face was like the face of an angel.*"

When you have the guts to praise the Lord, when you have the guts to open yourself up fully to Jesus, when you surrender your life to Him, you will reflect Him. Your beauty will be his beauty, and everyone who sees you is going to notice it from the start.

The closer you get to Jesus, the brighter you get! The closer Jesus got to the cross, the more the crowd left him or turned against him, until even his friends ran away. The same is true of us. If you start to reflect, if you start to glow, if you start to meet God more and more, some of your friends are going to run. Some of your popularity might get bruised a little. When you start to really look into the face of Jesus, the hymn that says, "The things of earth will grow strangely dim in the light of His glory and grace," becomes real. Do you have the courage to seek after Him and catch a glimpse of his power unleashed in your life? Do you have the courage to see the Lord's beauty and watch your face take on a radical new appearance? Do you have the courage to look into the very face of your savior Jesus Christ? When we spend time with the Master, we always walk away changed. Prayer, private worship, corporate worship, and Bible study all bring us closer to God. In all of these things we are worshiping our king. We learn, we grow, we gain a better understanding of Him, and we come away different than when we started.

The last thing David asks for is to seek him in his temple. If you are a Christian, if you have been saved, if you have Jesus into your heart, then guess what? You are his temple. So, what is it David is seeking? He is seeking the Lord's will and direction for his life. He had seen the beauty of God; he had dwelt in the house of the Lord, now out of pure love for God. David wanted to go where the Lord told him to go, and do what the Lord told him to do. The first thing we have to do is let Jesus clean us up. We can't hold anything back if we are going to be real. John the Baptist pointed to the coming of Jesus, saying in Matthew 3:11, "I baptize you with water unto repentance: he shall baptize you with the Holy Spirit, and with fire."

In Isaiah 6, when Isaiah looks into the face of God, he cries out "I am undone"; it was a cry of pain. When looking face to face into the eyes of God, he realized just how sinful he really was. The question in seeking the Lord is not where God wants me to go college or whom does he want me to date. It is the awareness of the sin in our lives. Our sin stops our worship dead in its tracks. You can't enter into God's temple if you are covered in the all the mud and dirt of your life outside of the temple. Isaiah was a mess, and he became aware of it. The Bible says it took a live coal to remove his guilt and sin touched his tongue. If we really seek Him, we have to be ready to lose a little bit. We have to be ready to give up some areas of our life that need to be burned away. It might hurt a little, too. The road to Jesus isn't easy, and it isn't all fun and games. It's the only way to survive, and if you want to live the life your Creator planned for you, it is your only choice.

David knew there was a price to be paid for following God. He knew that it would not be easy. But he also knew the results would be so much greater in the hands of God than in the hands of men. Steven Curtis Chapman recently wrote a song where he asks the question: "Where else could I be, and where else could I go? All I have been made for, there is nowhere else I could go, I am found in you."

Are you found in Him? Do you reflect the light of God in your face, because you have met Him face to face? Can you really worship Him? Do you know your love for Jesus is for real?

> And you, my son Solomon, acknowledge the God of your father and serve him with wholehearted devotion and with a willing mind, for the Lord searches every heart and understands every motive behind the thoughts. If you seek him, he will be found by you,

> if you reject him, he will reject you forever. Consider now, for the Lord has chosen you to build a temple as a sanctuary. Be strong and do the work.
>
> —1 Chronicles 28:9

Christian, salvation occurs in an instant, but living your life for and through Jesus takes a lifetime. Do you know how to worship him? It isn't hard. At its root, it is simply telling Him you love him, spending time with Him, and crying out to Him to keep working through you. If you are not ashamed of Him, then you want to live for him!

> Better is one day in your courts than a thousand elsewhere; I would rather be a doorkeeper in the house of my God than dwell in the tents of the wicked.
>
> —Psalm 84:10

Fulfilling the Destiny of Worship

Setting the spark. . . .

Do you have the guts to praise the Lord? Do you have the courage to enter into the throne room of God? Do you have the desire to know Jesus enough that you will open yourself up to Him, allowing him access to all of those areas of your life that you keep for yourself? You see that is what worship is. Worship and praise of God is crying out to him, seeking him, loving him, and bringing your heart and mind into His presence.

Have I ever really experienced worship?

What is holding me back?

Do I really WANT to know God like that?

What am I afraid of?

Fanning the flame. . . .

Thousands of years ago, Israel had a king who knew how to

worship the Lord. He knew how "to love the Lord with all his heart, with all his soul, and with all his mind." His name was David, and there is much more to his life than just killing Goliath! David was the greatest king in Israel's history. He could not be stopped in battle, his country had the best economy of any in the world, he was a hero, and he is the only person in the Bible to be called a "man after God's own heart." He knew God's heart, because he allowed himself to worship. He knew God's heart because he realized that his strength came from being on his knees before God. He was the king, and he had every thing he could ever want. But what David wanted most of all is found in *PSALM 27:4–14*.

What three things did David want most of all?

1. To dwell ____
2. To gaze ____
3. To seek ____

Psalm 84:4 says that *Blessed are those who dwell in your house; they are ever praising you*. We can't even praise and worship in a service for twenty minutes without getting distracted or worrying about what someone else might think. But the Bible says we should be "ever praising." Ephesians 3:17 says that so *Christ may dwell in your hearts through faith*. If you want to dwell in the house of the Lord, you need look no further than your own heart. People that see God have a different appearance. Psalm 34:5 says that *those who look to him are RADIANT!* Its time to stop treating worship as singing a few songs. Its time to make our lives an act of worship: "*ever praising You*." It is time for you to meet Jesus face to face in your life. You think the world has something better? You think that drugs, or sex, or alcohol, or parties, or popularity or girlfriends will fill your life? Is being devoted to Jesus going to cost you too much? Is there a part of you that thinks the world still has something that is better than Jesus? Look at David. He had everything.

Talk about living the good life: You got a car? David had dozens of chariots to get him around. You got a girlfriend or boyfriend? David had a dozen wives! He has you beat on wealth, fame, and anything else you could think of . . . but here is where it counts:

Psalm 84:10: Better is one day in your courts than a thousand elsewhere; I would rather be a doorkeeper in the house of my God than dwell in the tents of the wicked.

He had it all. None of it mattered. Being with God, worshiping God is all he wanted to do. Is worship important to you? If worship is just singing songs, then you have missed one of the greatest and most vital parts of the Christian life.

IGNITE THE PASSION. . . .

You know what happens when we see God face to face? You know what happens when you really forget about the rest of the room and focus on God? You know what happens when you REALLY worship? Your appearance changes.

David talks about "gazing on the beauty of the Lord," *and* "seeking Him in His temple." *You know what happens to people in the Bible after they see God?*

1. Exodus 34:29 . . . What happens to Moses?

____

____

____

2. 2 Corinthians 3:18 . . . Where does the "glow" come from?

____

____

____

3. Matthew 17:2 . . . What did Stephen look like?

____

____

____

It's simple! The closer you get to Jesus, the brighter you are going to shine! When you allow yourself to worship, when you allow yourself to open up to Him, when you start to tell Him how much you love him, you will reflect Him!

Living a life walking with Jesus is not about just reading the Bible and praying. It's about a deeply personal relationship with God, through Jesus. Relationships require communication! They require time! They require expressing love! In our relationship with Jesus, that is what worship is. Tell him how much you love Him, in every area of your life.

READ PSALM 139, then read it again, this time as your prayer to God: a prayer of worship.

Wide Awake

And do this, understanding the present time. The hour has come for you to wake up from your slumber, because our salvation is nearer now then we first believed. The night is nearly over; the day is almost here. So let us put aside the deeds of darkness and put on the armor of light.

—Romans 13:11–12 (NIV)

The term, "wake from our slumber" translates "rise to reality." Our world today has a pretty brutal reality to awaken to. The University of Michigan, in a 1993 study, found that by the eighth grade, 67 percent of youth say they have tried alcohol, 13 percent marijuana, and 45 percent have smoked cigarettes. Sexual behavior starts earlier and earlier. When asked what they believe spiritually, most teens that I meet say that there are no moral absolutes, and God is how you define it. Divorce, single-parent homes, drug abuse, suicide, school shootings, and date rape have all become commonplace terms to the students of today. Sexually transmitted diseases have increased to such an extent that schools now hand out condoms to keep the situation under control. Even in the church, the world system seems to have taken control. In one particular youth group that I am familiar with, there have been problems with marijuana, suicide attempts, cigarette smoking, alcohol and sex; and these are the regularly attending students, whose parents are active in the church!

My friends, there is another reality to awaken to as well: God is still on his throne, Jesus still saves and changes lives, and we can rise above all the world can throw at us through a personal relationship with Jesus Christ. Do you realize that every day brings us one day closer to the moment that Jesus will return for His church? That is what Paul is telling us when he says, "Our salvation is nearer now than when we first believed," and "This night is nearly over." We can't sit by and let the world go on! We can't hide in our churches and pretend that everything is fine. Paul tells us to put "on the armor of light." That, to me, says we had better get into the battle. We don't need armor if we are hiding in the castle. We need the armor to engage the enemy. Your friends are lost and desperate, and you carry around with you all day the hope that can set them free. Do you just brush aside Jesus in exchange for the "deeds of darkness," or are you ready to get up, put on the armor, and get into the battle? It is time for this generation to wake up.

In Romans 12:11, Paul uses the word "zeal" to describe how our service to the Lord should be. You know what that means? It translates to "boiling." We are to be "boiling with the Spirit of God." What happens when a pot of water boils? It expands and expands until it spills out of its container. When you catch the true fire of God, and embrace his destiny for you, you won't be able to contain the Spirit of God in your life. Jeremiah calls it a "fire shut up in his bones," that he cannot, nor does not want to keep in. Youth groups, churches, and individual Christians cannot exist inside the church walls. The church of Jesus Christ only becomes the church He intended when it is active out in the world!

> What I mean, brothers, is that the time is short. From now on, those who have wives should live as if they had none; those who mourn, as if they did not; those who are happy, as if they were not, those who buy something, as if it were not theirs to keep; those who use the things of the world, as if not engrossed in them. For this world, in its present form, is passing away.
>
> —1 Corinthians 7:29–31 (NIV)

Paul is not telling us to divorce our wives and give up all of our belongings. What he is saying is that we need to WAKE UP! We need to realize that this world will not last and the focus of our lives should be on the things that really matter: our relationship with Jesus, and the spreading of His word. Paul is pleading with you to realize the seriousness of life, and the vital role that you play in your place in the world. According to Jerry Falwell, 95 percent of the people who become Christians do so by the age of 21. Yet, the average church spends less than 2 percent of its resources on that age group. That places you on the greatest mission field the world has ever known: your own school, your own job, and your own neighborhood!

If you are a student, then you are on a mission field, as critical to the cause of Christ as anywhere else in the world! What is the difference? In public schools today, the government wants to stop you from sharing your faith, there is the chance of violence, you are abused and taunted by the "natives of the land," and every single day you encounter people who know nothing about Jesus Christ. Tell me what the difference is! It is time we were wide-awake to the reality of our world. The time is getting shorter, and the night is almost over! We must be about the business of God's destiny for our lives. It is an old cliché, but it still applies: You may be the only Jesus that someone ever sees.

> Arise from the depression and prostration in which your circumstances have kept you—rise to a new life. Shine and be radiant with the glory of the Lord, for your light has come and the glory of the Lord has risen upon you.
>
> —Isaiah 60:1 (Amplified)

This verse can be summed up in one sentence: wake up and get up. Now if God is telling these people to "get up," then they must be sitting down. They are our basic American churches.

They are getting by, hanging around, pleasing themselves, and not getting anything accomplished for God. Now God is saying, "Get up!" He cries out to them, "I have placed my glory upon you, I have saved you, I have made you my bride so start acting like it!" The Bible says that Jesus is coming back like a groom coming to claim his bride. Think about that. If you left your bride, as a young, lean, beautiful girl, then came back to find that she had never cleaned the house, eaten Twinkies all day, and gained about fifty pounds, would you feel the trip was worth it? God is saying to us its time to get out of the mindset that we are weak and powerless. Get out of the idea that you can't do anything. Stop being a victim and become a victor! Step off the sidelines, drop your fear, and get out into the world to share with them a message that they desperately need to hear!

God did not heal you up, rescue you, clean you up, set you free and give you a new life so that you could take that light and hide it in a church building! He means for you to shine that light into every dark corner you can find! In case you haven't noticed, most people are fed up with professional religion. They are fed up with marriages that fail, friends who betray them, and families that don't stick together. They are fed up with a world that tells them they are useless without this hairstyle, or that clothing brand. They are fed up with leaders who fail and make a mockery of honor. They are fed up with people who offer them every type of answer to life, only to find it leaves them more empty than when they started!

These people, the people you come into contact with every day need to know that Jesus is real, alive, and living inside of someone who cares about them! If Jesus has ever done anything for you, if He has ever set you free from hurt, depression, drugs, alcohol, pornography, hate, or mistakes from your past, then you have a message that a whole lost and dying world needs to hear! All of the activities, pizza parties, and camps in the world won't reach your friends. You have to reach them. The greatest tool for reaching the lost is a heart so filled with the love of God, it is infectious.

God is ready to set a fire on a generation that is ready to wake up and put on the armor He has entrusted to us. The Bible says that Jesus is "the same, yesterday, today, and forever." That being the case, if we are not seeing the powerful church that we see in the Bible, then it must be we who have become lazy and ineffective.

In Acts 2, we see a church that is on fire. We see a group of people who will not be stopped. A group of people who will shout from the rooftops, "Jesus is Lord." People like to say, "That was the biblical times . . . things are different now." Yeah they are; they are worse. The Bible says over and over that God doesn't change! If He hasn't, then His church has! We need to awaken to the reality that God wants to set an all-consuming fire inside of us! He is waiting for a generation that will not settle for just getting by. A generation that worships, prays, and witnesses with a fire that is shut up in their bones! A fire so hot, they cannot contain it, nor keep it in.

In Acts 2, there was such a powerful move of God that is was PHYSICALLY felt all over town. The Bible says there was a wind and an earthquake that was so strong it rocked the whole city. People came out in the streets wondering what had happened. They found the apostles preaching in the streets in all of these different languages. They ridiculed them, claiming they were drunk at nine in the morning. Did that stop the apostles? No. They preached on, consumed by the fire of their God, and that day 3,000 people were saved. The next day, the number grew to 5,000. Throughout the Book of Acts, we see these men rocking their world for God.

> Acts 4:31 . . . after they prayed, the place in which they were assembled was shaken; and they were all filled with the Holy Spirit,

and they continued to speak the word of God with **freedom, boldness, and courage.**

Acts 5:28 . . . we charged you not to teach in or about his name; yet here you have flooded Jerusalem with your doctrine.

Acts 17:5 . . . these men who have turned the world upside down, have now come here also.

If we are not going to believe that we can have the same freedom, boldness, and courage then we might as well quit now. If we are not going to believe that "I can do ALL things through Christ who strengthens me," then we should throw away our Bibles and never open them again. Jesus is both exactly whom He said he was, and every word of His Bible is true, or it is all the mad ranting of a lunatic. Either there is "power in the blood," or we are all wasting our time on a fraud.

I am so tired of being around depressed, visionless, powerless people. God is looking for a people who are hungry for change: a people who have had enough of the status quo. A people who are ready to discover the destiny that God has meticulously crafted and formed each of them, individually. Why would we want to go back to Egypt, when the Promised Land is just on the other side of the desert?

There is a great story in Matthew about the disciples out in a boat during a storm. They had just spent hours with Jesus, but now they felt like He had left them. Then they see Him out on the water. Peter decides to head out into the water after his king. He starts walking on the water, then realizes what is happening, and begins to sink. He calls out to Jesus, and Jesus picks him up. So often, I hear people use this story to criticize Peter for a lack of faith. Let me ask you this: where were the rest of the disciples? I would rather sink in the water going after Jesus than be dry in a boat of do-nothing, indecisive people.

If I look back on the last ten years of my life, I am amazed. I have had the experience of traveling all over the world. I have worked, dined with, and been in the homes of many famous people. I have witnessed, firsthand, Jesus transforming many lives. I have had the privilege of speaking in front of hundreds of teenagers and telling them the same things I am sharing with you in this book. God's road is exactly what Steven Curtis Chapman called it: a great adventure. I never would have believed the path if you had shown it to me in advance, but I am so grateful to my Savior for building it just for me. My hope for this book is that you will embrace the great adventure of living for God. I have never met anyone who regretted following Jesus. It is your destiny. It is what you are built for. Nobody loves you more than Jesus Christ, and there is no greater life than a life spent walking on the water after Him.

> Therefore I tell you, do not worry about your life, what will eat; or about your body, what you will wear. Life is more than food and the body more than clothes. Consider the ravens: they do not sow or reap, they have no storeroom or barn; yet God feeds them. And how much more valuable you are than birds!
>
> —Luke 12:22–24

Fulfilling the Destiny of No Compromise

Setting the spark. . . . Paul tells us throughout Romans that we need to be aware of the world around us. We should understand who we are in Christ, what the world is like, and our mission in this world. Paul was sold out to Jesus. He understood the reality of the world he lived in and the importance of his message.

Read Galatians 1:10.

1. What was Paul's evidence that he was not interested in pleasing man?

 ____

2. Whose approval was Paul interested in?

____

Fanning the flame. . . . Paul did not weaken or change his message for anyone. He was unwilling to try to remove the parts of the Gospel that people might be offended by. It wasn't that he was the greatest preacher who ever lived. It wasn't that he had money or good looks. What made Paul so effective was a total commitment to the truth. John MacArthur said, "He was Christ's ambassador, not his press secretary." Paul's message could never be negotiated. He didn't soften it to fit the attitudes of the day.

Read Romans 1:16. *The gospel is power. The message of Christ is powerful. It has the power to save, to heal, and to set free. List three times this week when you have denied the power of the gospel and found yourself ashamed instead.*

1. ____

____

2. ____

____

3. ____

____

Read Romans 13:11–12

1. What is Paul telling us that we must leave behind in order to respond to the urgency of the times that we are living in?

____

2. List three things in your life that could be thought of as "deeds of darkness" that are causing you to lose your focus on the truth of the Gospel.
3. ____
4. ____
5. ____

Igniting a passion. Paul tells us in Romans 13:14 that we should focus our lives on Jesus, and ignore "the desires of the sinful nature." If we are going to make a difference for Christ in this world, then we need to start spending time focusing on Him, and not the car, the video game, or the girl sitting next to us in class.

List below five lost friends. They should be people whom you have contact with on a daily basis. Pray for these five people, by name, each and every morning, at night before you go to bed, and at lunch. Pray for their salvation, and for you to have the opportunity to witness to them. By making their salvation your focus, your mind will automatically focus more and more on Christ. Study the plan of salvation in the back of this book, and be ready, for the time is now.

1. ______________________________
2. ______________________________
3. ______________________________
4. ______________________________
5. ______________________________

Notes

Notes

Notes

Notes